Project Teams

Project Teams

A Structured Development Approach

Vittal S. Anantatmula

Project Teams: A Structured Development Approach

First published in 2016 by
Business Expert Press, LLC
222 East 46th Street, New York, NY 10017
www.businessexpertpress.com

ISBN-13: 978-1-63157-162-6 (paperback)
ISBN-13: 978-1-63157-163-3 (e-book)

Business Expert Press Portfolio and Project Management Collection

Collection ISSN: 2156-8189 (print)
Collection ISSN: 2156-8200 (electronic)

Cover and interior design by Exeter Premedia Services Private Ltd., Chennai, India

First edition: 2016

10 9 8 7 6 5 4 3 2 1

Printed in the United States of America.

I dedicate this book to all those who contributed immensely to my personal and professional growth: family, friends, teachers, professors, and students. I continue to learn from all of them.

Abstract

Projects generally require skills and effort from multiple disciplines to develop project deliverables. Projects are executed in teams, as project tasks require multiple skills, judgment, and experience. In a project, the roles of teams should be assigned based on strengths of individuals.

In a project, the *team process* is a mediating mechanism that links variables such as members, team, and organizational characteristics, which include structure, culture, supporting systems, performance and incentive systems, employee morality, and top management support.

Team performance or teamwork is impacted by the structure of a team. A team's structural characteristics include the number of team members, the status hierarchy, roles and responsibilities, and accepted norms for behaviors of individuals within the team. Furthermore, understanding the characteristics of virtual teams and their key attributes for improving global project performance are of critical importance.

Social and behavioral skills that each person brings are important influencing factors in interactions with other team members and in forming a cohesive and productive team. Also, organization and national cultures influence a team member's performance. Furthermore, many generations from Baby Boomers to Generation Y work together in the workplace today.

Project Teams is a book that attempts to address all these topics in detail and offer a practical approach to managing projects successfully in the current business environment by including concepts, processes, techniques, and tools to manage and enhance performance of project teams and projects. This book would be meaningful for project management professionals and project managers in any organization and can be a useful resource for academic institutions in teaching management and project management disciplines.

Keywords

global projects, projects, project management, project management maturity, project teams, social and behavioral skills for teams, teams, teamwork, team performance, team process, virtual teams

Contents

Preface

The very basis of forming organizations is to bring people together for working on common goals. Organizations are generally managed through creation of divisions, departments, and teams for productivity gains and collaborative efforts. Among these, teams are more productive, flexible, and responsive to change.

The *Project Teams* book is written for graduate students in business and engineering schools, project management professionals, project managers, and senior executives of any organization. Many managers and executives are involved in developing teams, team processes, and managing them for productivity gains. Although there is ample study and research on teams in disciplines such as sociology, social psychology, organizational behavior, and management, project teams face unique challenges. From the perspective of all these disciplines, this book addresses specific challenges associated with projects and the ways to manage them successfully.

Projects are vehicles for organizations to meet their strategic objectives and operational goals, and they are executed in teams. As such, being a member of a team is an inevitable feature of modern work life. A project team comprises a selected group of individuals with complementary skills and disciplines, who are required to work together on interdependent and interrelated tasks for a predetermined period to meet a specific purpose or goal. Project teams can be traditional colocated teams, virtual teams, and global project teams. Common purpose, goal, interdependence due to mutual accountability and collective responsibility, diverse skills, information sharing, and collaborative efforts characterize project teams.

Uncertainty, uniqueness, complexity, and unfamiliarity are often associated with projects and, as a result, the project manager and the project team are compelled to deal with change. Consequently, successful project performance requires strong leadership, which provides vision and ability to cope with change. Furthermore, efforts are made to align individual aspirations and goals with the project goals, thereby creating synergy, creativity, and participative decision making. Global projects present challenges of political, cultural, virtual, and regional differences. A more formal approach to team development and management processes is necessary and knowledge management and communication are key aspects of global project teams.

The *Project Teams* book provides an overview of selecting, structuring, developing, and managing project teams. It provides a detailed account of team-development approaches and processes that deal with social and behavioral issues, decision making, conflict resolution, communication, motivation, knowledge sharing, and lessons for continuous improvement. The book also discusses about practices of high performing and successful project teams that lay emphasis on improving cohesion using team charter and by addressing social and behavioral issues to build emotional intelligence and making them self-managed teams.

Vittal S. Anantatmula
Western Carolina University

Acknowledgments

Success comes with teamwork. A desire to share my knowledge is the inspiration for this research effort and for choosing this topic for the book, as it is evident that people working together could make a difference and contribute significantly to the success of projects and organizations. I received encouragement from Dr. Timothy Kloppenborg, editor of the book series, and I am grateful to him. My wife, Manga, was patient and supportive throughout this research effort and encouraged me to focus on my research by taking care of many personal issues and challenges during this period. Many thanks to Dr. Parviz Rad, Dr. Edward Wright, Dr. Tracey Richardson, and my graduate assistant, Matthew Smith, for reviewing the draft and providing useful suggestions.

CHAPTER 1

Significance of Teams

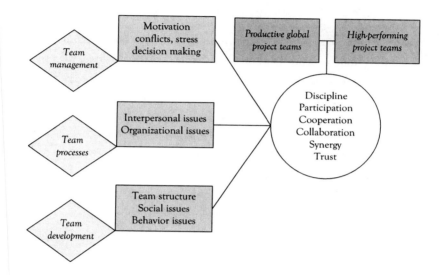

Objectives:

- Understand what project teams are and how they can be implemented.
- Learn the impact project teams can have on an organization.
- Recognize the relationship between the project life cycle and project team cycle.
- Realize the project team development stages.

Preview

In this chapter, the focus is on the basic structure and characteristics of teams and the impact that teams have on operational efficiency and effectiveness. The chapter begins by explaining the difference between different groups, including their formation and degree of cohesiveness. The chapter illustrates the different strata of groups, and their position in the workplace. Project teams receive the most emphasis, and the life cycle of project teams is explained so that readers can effectively harness the power of project teams in the future. The development of teams is highlighted due to the integral nature of group origination.

Introduction

Being a member of a team is the norm of work life and it is unavoidable. The ability to work with other individuals and in teams is a critical competency that employers often look for in hiring decisions. Perhaps, one may think that only discipline-specific skills are considered for selection and recruitment. However, selection on the basis of technical skills alone may be a thing of the past. Good organizations look for one's ability to work with others collaboratively, and to communicate effectively. Discipline-specific skills are essential but not sufficient. Studies show that people lose their jobs often for lack of interpersonal skills.

Google senior management says that behavioral attributes, not scholastic aptitude test (SAT) scores and grade point average (GPA) are considered important in making recruitment decisions. Research suggests that adaptability, social and emotional intelligence, resilience, friendliness, and raw intelligence are considered important in selecting employees. Knack is a Silicon Valley startup that uses games with advanced data analysis to identify characteristics of successful and innovative employees. Knack chief executive officer Guy Halfteck says,

> … social abilities, being able to intelligently manage the social landscape, intelligently respond to other people, read the social situation and reason with social savviness—this turns out to differentiate between people who do better and people who don't do as well.[1]

---

[1] Nisen (2013).

The very basis of forming organizations is to bring people together to work for a common purpose. Organizations are managed through formation of divisions, departments, task forces, and teams for efficiency and effectiveness. When referring to people working together in an organization or outside of it, these collaborative efforts are often referred to terms such as groups and teams. A recent study[2] suggests that successful organizations encourage informal and collaborative relationships, thereby promoting team culture at the organization level.

Groups

Groups come together either in an organization or outside of it. A group consists of two or more people with a common relationship. Community groups for voluntary services, for fun, or social cause (sports fans or fan clubs, associations) are often formed outside formal corporate structures. Groups are integral to our lives and provide security, and opportunities to interact socially, manage complexity, bring people together, and facilitate an exchange of knowledge.

Voluntary group or union is the most commonly found nonprofit group outside the organizational context. It is a group of individuals who enter into an agreement willingly as volunteers to form an association to accomplish a specific purpose. Research has shown that volunteering has mental and physical health benefits such as improving your mood, making you feel healthier, increasing your sense of purpose, and reducing your stress levels. Volunteering can also give us a deep sense of happiness, both immediately and in long term.[3] Some of the famous volunteering groups are Red Cross, Peace Corps, Amnesty International, Make a Wish Foundation, and People for Ethical Treatment of Animals (PETA).

---

[2] Towers Watson (2014).

[3] projecthelping.org

In an organizational context, a group can also be formal or informal, official or unofficial, task oriented or relationship oriented or both, permanent or temporary, and colocated or physically dispersed. Divisions and departments can be termed as formal groups, and they are often associated with formal structures such as business organizations and associations. Informal groups such as communities of practice and informal networks, in addition to formal work groups, are often integral to organizations.

- *Communities of practice* are formed to support each other and develop the capabilities of their members. Individual members have a choice to join this group due to passion, commitment, or expertise in a specific discipline. This group is not bound by time.
- *Informal networks* are formed within organizations for mutual needs and support. Members support each other by sharing business information. In many cases, informal networks are as effective as formal groups in delivering organizational goals. Informal networks are also not time bound.
- *Formal groups* are created to deliver products or services. Members become part of the formal group due to their job responsibilities and often report to the group's leader or manager to facilitate working toward a common goal.

Outside formal organization structures, the business-oriented, social networking service LinkedIn facilitates more professional and informal groups, such as communities of practice and informal networks, than any other social media. If the question "what's in it for me" is not addressed well, it is difficult to populate a group on LinkedIn. The groups in LinkedIn facilitate exchanging ideas, answering questions, mentoring other members in the group, and sharing knowledge. Helping others is the key aspect if the content and content quality are managed well. Group members will get an opportunity to learn from senior professionals in the group, engage with the professional community, pursue their interests, and find employment opportunities.

People with common interests and similar attitudes tend to join informal networks voluntarily and work together to help each other and increase job satisfaction. Although informal social interactions are voluntary, research suggests that the organizational structure influences the structure of informal networks. National cultures also influence the structure, incidence, and cohesiveness of informal structures. It is easy and natural to form informal networks in countries like Japan and India, whereas it could be different in individualistic societies like the United States.

Informal networks transfer information that gives rise to attitude similarity, imitation, and the generation of innovations. Additionally, such networks mediate transactions among organizations, cooperation among persons, and give differential access to resources and power.[4] One must remember that informal networks can have both positive and negative impact on the organization.

The most natural and common informal group is the family. Informal groups are not often governed by externally imposed rules and regulations although social norms prevail. In general, informal groups set their own governing principles and goals. Every one of us belongs to a group or a few informal groups.

Working groups in organizations consist of people who do not necessarily depend on each other and do not share a common goal. However, working groups share information and knowledge to do their jobs better.

Teams

Teams are usually comprised of a small number of people with complementary skills working together with a common purpose and commitment toward a goal. A team always has a shared obligation or commitment. We find various definitions of a team in the literature (Table 1.1).

From the definitions listed in the Table 1.1, one can identify a few common factors of a team such as common purpose or goal, interdependence due to mutual accountability and collective responsibility, diverse skills, information sharing, and collaborative efforts. A team is *a selected group of individuals with diverse and complimentary skills who are required*

---

[4] Brass et al. (2004).

Table 1.1 Team definitions

Definition	Source
A team is "a group of individuals with mutual accountability that work interdependently to solve problems or carry out work."	Kirkman and Mathieu (2005, 701)
A team is "a group of individuals who work together under a unity of purpose, as a united front."	Kezsbom (1995, 480)
A team is "a small number of people with complimentary skills who are committed to a common purpose, set of performance goals, and approach for which they hold themselves mutually accountable."	Katzenbach and Smith (1993, 112)
A team is "a collection of individuals who are interdependent in their tasks, who share responsibility for outcomes, who see themselves and who are seen by others as an intact social entity embedded in one or more larger social systems, and who manage their relationship across organizational boundaries."	Cohen and Bailey (1997, 241)
Teaming is "an act that occurs whenever two or more people communicate with each other, formally or informally, in an enabling environment characterized by individual innovation and collective consensus."	Shuster (1999, 196)

to work together collaboratively for a predetermined period and are collectively responsible to meet a specific purpose or goal.

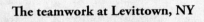

The teamwork at Levittown, NY

"First came the trucks. Every 100 feet, they would dump precisely bundled packages of lumber, piping, and other building supplies, then pour a concrete slab foundation. Then came the men. Working in teams of two or three in a precise, 26-step choreography, the framers, the painters, the installers, the electricians, and so on would do their assigned task—and move on to the next home, over and over. At the peak of production, the building teams could complete 36 homes a day. The result was Levittown, NY, America's first mass-produced suburb. Henry Ford, who died a few months before ground was broken, would have appreciated the simple genius of this reverse assembly line. In Levittown, it was the workers who moved, not the product.

From 1947 to 1951, the Levitt family built 17,500 houses. A typical ranch cost $7,990. On one August day in 1949, sales reps sold 650 houses in five hours. Levittown pioneered building techniques that are now standard—and helped to bring the American dream of home ownership within reach of thousands of people of modest means. And no, it never became a slum."

—By Cait Murphy

Source: Secrets of Greatness: Great Teams. *Fortune Magazine*, May 31, 2006, http://archive.fortune.com/2006/05/31/magazines/fortune/six-teams_greatteams_fortune_061206/index.htm

Teams could be categorized into six types:[5] (1) project, (2) production, (3) service, (4) action/performing, (5) management, and (6) parallel. The first four teams are temporal to a great extent and adapt planning, strategy, and goal-setting approaches, whereas management and parallel team activities involve analyzing situations, formulating strategies, and setting goals.[6]

From a different perspective, teams are formed to recommend actions, execute tasks, or manage operations in organizations. Recommending actions is often assigned to a task force. Project and manufacturing tasks are associated with executing or doing things. A variety of teams are

---

[5] Sundstrom (1999).

[6] Marks, Mathieu, and Zaccaro (2001).

Table 1.2 Types of teams definitions

Definition	Source
Virtual team comprises of individuals who are geographically and/or organizationally dispersed, working together through telecommunication to accomplish organizational tasks.	Townsend, DeMarie, and Hendrickson (1998)
Multicultural team is "a group of people from different cultures, with a joint deliverable for the organization or the stakeholder."	Stahl et al. (2010, 439)
Distributed team is "groups of geographically dispersed employees with a common goal carrying out interdependent tasks using mostly technology for communication and collaboration."	Bosch-Sijtsema, Ruohomäki, and Vartiainen (2009, 534)

found in organizations such as global teams, virtual teams, distributed teams, and global project teams. Definitions of broad categories of teams are included in Table 1.2.

Distinction Between Groups and Teams

Unlike groups, teams are not generally formed voluntarily. They are explicitly designed and developed to meet specific goals of the organization. So, teams usually exist in formal organization structures. Needless to say, the organization's structure, culture, power, authority, and politics influence a team's effectiveness and productivity.

Groups are usually formed on a long-term basis as compared to teams, and they last much longer than teams. Teams are disbanded after the goal is achieved. For example, a team comprising of several team members, assigned for an airport construction project, is assigned to new projects or tasks once the airport construction is complete, whereas the airport operations group is formed during the final stages of its construction and continues to function as a group as long as the airport is providing service to airlines and commuters.

Compared to groups, a team always has a common goal. Furthermore, teams are distinct as compared to other groups; a team is characterized by a group of individuals for their accountability, specific roles and responsibilities, interdependent and interrelated tasks, and collective performance. Also, teams can be quickly assembled, deployed, refocused,

Table 1.3 Groups and teams

Groups	Teams
Focused, strong leader	Shared and collective leadership
Individual responsibility and accountability	Individual and collective accountability
Group and organization's purposes are same	Team purpose is different from that of the organization
Structured and efficient meetings	Open-ended and problem-solving meetings
Individual performance and outcome	Collective performance and outcome
Long-term duration	Teams are disbanded after achieving the goal

Source: Adapted from Katzenbach and Smith (1993).

and disbanded. The essential features of teams and groups are captured in Table 1.3.

The nature and reason for the formation of a group or team would influence its cohesiveness and effectiveness. Imagine being part of the team for planning and organizing the Tokyo 2020 Olympics! Expectations and support from the public and businesses within Japan would be very high. The team's motivation, collaboration, cohesiveness, and commitment would be at a very high level, as one cannot imagine a bigger and more prestigious project than the Olympics.

Unlike teams, groups do not necessarily engage in collective work that requires interdependent effort. Therefore, all teams are groups but not all groups are teams. Teams focus on both individual and collective performance and discipline, whereas other forms of groups rely on individuals for group performance.

Project Teams

A project team comprises *a selected group of individuals with complimentary skills and disciplines who are required to work together on interdependent and interrelated tasks for a predetermined period to meet a specific purpose or goal.*

Project teams are formed to accomplish a specific project goal or a task and these teams are temporary. The senior management, project management office (PMO), or sometimes the project manager/leader select the project team members to work toward a common purpose or goal. It is important for project teams to work together well, and team synergy is of critical importance. Once the project is complete, the team members are assigned to other projects and the team is disbanded.

Project teams can be traditional colocated teams, virtual teams, and global project teams. Virtual teams are geographically dispersed either nationally or internationally, whereas global project teams are often virtual teams in which team members are dispersed geographically across national boundaries. In both cases, interaction and communication among the project teams take place electronically. The geographical distance in a virtual team can vary widely. Sometimes, people from different divisions of the same organization, located in different buildings, can be part of a virtual team.

Global projects employ virtual teams, and the project manager must lead these teams by playing a directive role predominantly and establishing clearly defined processes. The leadership role must be established first and clearly defined processes help in establishing trust. Decision making presents challenges due to culture-tampered varying approaches and styles. Finally, communicating electronically requires higher competency levels in written communication and reading comprehension.

Importance of Project Teams

Being a member of a group or team is an inevitable feature of modern work life. Being a member of a team is essential for projects and project management. Project teams are required for the organization to be more productive, flexible, and responsive to change.

Projects are vehicles for organizations to meet their strategic goals of growth, innovation, expansion of business, entry to new markets, new product development, and so forth. In the current global economy, organizations are bound to deliver products and services faster, better, and cheaper due to increased competition in the marketplace. Furthermore, organizations are motivated to reduce hierarchy for productivity gains and effectiveness. Consequently, organization structures are becoming lean and flat, which compel them to delegate authority and responsibility. Also, the global economy compels organizations to deal with complex problems and increased complexity in decision making. Under these circumstances, individuals acting alone may no longer have enough knowledge and skills to make decisions. These challenges underscore the importance of project teams.

Projects are executed in teams that aim for outcomes, which demand skills and expertise from multiple disciplines. Project management generally requires skills from disciplines that include but are not limited to organizational behavior, management, human resources, quality assurance, quantitative methods, finance, accounting, information systems, entrepreneurship, innovation, marketing, and economics. As projects demand multiple skills and discipline to improve success and enhance performance, project teams typically outperform individuals.

In general, projects are managed using teams in a complex work environment for two reasons: first, each project is unique, and second, conditions for team selection and motivation are often far from ideal. Uniqueness contributes to issues such as unknowns, uncertainties, technical complexity, and risk. Bringing together a group of people to collaborate for a cohesive effort presents many people-related challenges such as interpersonal relations and behavioral issues. In addition to uniqueness and complexity, unfamiliarity is often described as one of the characteristics of projects and as a result, projects are often associated with change and risk. Consequently, strong leadership, that provides vision and ability to cope with change, is a must for successful project performance.

Characteristics of Project Teams

Like any other team, a project team goes through phases of forming, storming, norming, performing, and adjourning. Transitioning from one phase to the other and time spent during each phase would depend on the organizational work culture, familiarity, and behavioral issues. Furthermore, the urgency (project schedule), complexity, unknowns, risks, and costs associated with the project also influence the team-development phases and transition.

Needless to say, project characteristics influence project team composition and characteristics. The leadership and management styles of the project manager during each of these phases would also be different. The project management life-cycle phases of initiation, planning, execution, monitoring and controlling, and closing would also influence project team development and management (Figure 1.1).

Furthermore, project team size would also depend on the project characteristics such as size of the project, technology, complexity, and diverse and complimentary skill set necessary to develop project deliverables. Although the size of many project teams falls within the normal team size range of 5 to 50 members, mega projects tend to have much larger project teams. Although teams outperform individuals, large project teams, often associated with mega projects, face several issues and constraints with respect to coordination and logistics. For example, one may have to deal with more people, thereby increasing the number of communication channels, more disciplines and functions, and coordination among greater numbers of individuals.

Often, selection of the project manager is based on having a high level of interpersonal and decision-making skills as managing people of diverse disciplines and skills for a coordinated and collaborative effort is very challenging. The need for diversity and expertise of team members and their selection would be determined by technical or functional expertise, problem-solving challenges, and decision-making skills required for project success. Interpersonal skills are equally important for project team selection.

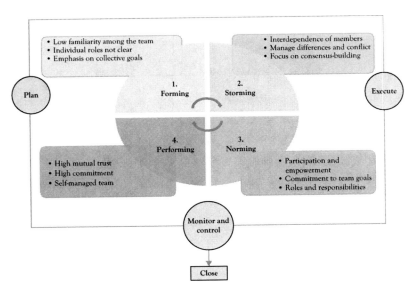

Figure 1.1 Project and team phases

Projects (and project teams) are also characterized by predetermined completion dates for their performance goals and tasks. Consequently, project teams cannot afford to delay the start of their teamwork and effective collaboration. Perhaps, it is one of the reasons why organizations encourage project teams to develop a team charter and responsibility matrix as quickly as practicable. It is also important for many project teams to transfer administrative and technical responsibility immediately after completing the project. Like any other team, project teams can be creative and productive by promoting participation, cooperation, and collaboration among the team members.

The project teams are also collectively accountable for project success and project management success. It is the responsibility of the team to complete the project on time, within budget, and develop project deliverables as per specifications while satisfying various key stakeholders. Therefore, project teams demand a strong sense of commitment to project goals.

Performance of Projects and Project Teams

Project success is comprised of standards or criteria that assess project outcomes or results. Over time, project success has evolved from narrow but universally accepted criteria of scope, cost, and time to include other criteria viewed from different perspectives. Additions include measures such as meeting enterprise strategic and financial objectives, and client and end-user satisfaction. These are broadly divided into internal and external factors. Internal project factors are the factors that the project manager and the project team control over time, cost, and performance. External client factors are usefulness, satisfaction, and effectiveness of the project outcome. However, these external success factors cannot be measured until the project is complete; the only way to assure them during the project execution, to a certain extent, is to understand client needs and translate them into specifications of the project deliverables.

In other words, project management success is viewed as the internal measure of efficiency, while project success is concerned with the project's external effectiveness. It is important to recognize that project management success factors of time, cost, and quality would also ensure project outcome success. Furthermore, one should recognize that project management success is a result of managing resources, specifically human resources. To state succinctly, the success of the project would include success of the implementation team in crafting the deliverable, together with the success of the enterprise in reaping benefits from the deliverable.

Project teams have a common purpose of delivering project outcomes within scope, time, and budget. Thus, the common purpose is translated into several performance goals. The common purpose tends to bind the team together, and performance goals motivate collaboration and synergy among the team members.

Project goals are unique to every project and these goals tend to be unambiguous, measurable, and tangible. Project goals that are defined with clarity facilitate project teams to perform better as a team, motivate individual team members, improve communication, and serve as a guiding light to manage conflicts. The more specific the performance goals are, the better it is to enhance overall team performance. For this to happen, project teams will have to spend enormous time in understanding client requirements and translating them into clearly defined specifications or attributes of project deliverables. Successful team approaches are listed in Table 1.4.

For any project team to adopt these successful team approaches, organizations and project team leaders have a lot of groundwork to do.

Developing Successful Project Teams

The purpose of this book is to provide an overview of selecting, structuring, developing, and managing project teams to improve collaborative effort and productivity in managing projects successfully.

A detailed exploration of team development is presented, including understanding social and behavioral issues and developing team processes to address such issues, and team management matters in regard to conflict resolution and stress management. All of these items are of importance in the development of high-performing project teams (Figure 1.2).

First, organizations should have culture to promote teamwork by structuring teams that support collaboration and synergy. A team structure design largely depends on the organization structure and organization

Table 1.4 Successful team approaches

Define roles and responsibilities, communicate expectations, establish urgency, and demand performance. Teams work better when they know what is expected of them unambiguously and by defining performance ethics. Creating compelling context would motivate them to work together and hard. Independence and accountability are considered important.
Focus on individual strengths, skill, skill potential, and personality. Team success depends on harnessing individual strengths, aspirations, skills, and personality. All these factors should be taken into consideration while assigning the role and responsibility of each team member. Efficiency and effectiveness are the goals.
Use initial meetings and actions to create cohesiveness. Initial meetings must be used to set informal ground rules. It is important to curb negative emotions to improve cohesiveness. Team lead must pay attention to curb negative emotions and encourage friendship among the team members.
Develop a team charter. To be successful as a team, it is important to set clear rules and norms by developing a team charter that outlines performance expectations and behavioral norms such as mutual respect, courtesy, collaboration, attendance, and communication protocol. Collaboration is the main focus.
Place importance on informal meetings. Project leader must facilitate casual and informal get-together meetings and encourage personal interactions to understand and, develop friendship among the team members. It would enhance collaborative efforts and cohesion.
Update the team with project progress. Project progress information and new challenges motivate the project team to step up their effort, collaboration, and synergy among the team members. Determination to accomplish project goals is critical.
Emphasize on positive feedback, recognition, and reward. Project leaders must recognize efforts that lead to successful performance. Recognition, reward, and work satisfaction are important to motivate team members for higher performance.

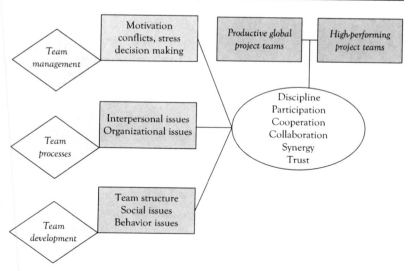

Figure 1.2 Project team efficacy model

culture. Furthermore, senior management must understand the importance of instilling a work culture that recognizes social and behavioral issues at an individual level and to transition individuals from self-identity to self-managed high-performance teams with higher levels of emotional intelligence. All these team structure and development issues are discussed at length in the next chapter.

Second, organizations must focus on developing and sustaining team-related processes that would ensure continuity and continual improvement in team development. A team process is a facilitating method of linking team variables—organizational characteristics such as structure, culture, supporting systems, performance and incentive systems, employee morality, and top management support—with the team and its members. Interactions and dependencies among all the team variables could become complex. Successful organizations develop these team processes and ensure smooth functioning of these processes along with knowledge sharing and knowledge transfer process to nurture individual learning, team learning, and organizational learning. Ultimately, these processes are aimed to develop highly productive teams and to nurture growth of individuals to become team leaders. Team-related processes are discussed in Chapter 3 of this book.

Third, project teams require both management and leadership as stress and conflicts are bound to occur in project teams initially. By aligning goals or aspirations of individual team members with the project goals, and by investing time in understanding individual strengths and weaknesses, the project manager would be in a better position to define roles and responsibilities of individual team members, communicate expectations with clarity, motivate and influence individuals to align their interests with project goals, develop trust and higher levels of commitment. Consequently, the focus will be on management and leadership roles to do things right and doing right things, respectively. Establishing trust is a slow process and the project manager should, in addition to management and leadership roles, play a supportive role in nurturing growth, sharing knowledge, and encouraging participation in the decision-making process. The goal is to divide the task and multiply the success of the project team. Issues related to managing and leading teams are discussed at length in Chapter 4.

Fourth, it is important to identify practices and processes that would lead to development of highly productive project teams. With the global economy and free market philosophy, global virtual projects are becoming the norm and traditional teams that are colocated and communicate face-to-face are likely to become nontraditional. However, successful and promising practices and processes that assure high performance are different for traditional global project teams and colocated teams. Global project teams rely on electronic communication but have the advantage of including talented team members from several regions in the world, often at low cost. However, global project teams face additional challenges of managing cultural differences, absence of nonverbal and face-to-face communication methods, and difficulty in leading teams across national boundaries that include different social, political, cultural, business, and legal environments. These different sets of promising practices for traditional and global project teams are aimed at improving cooperation, participation, and collaboration, thereby resulting in higher levels of synergy, trust, motivation, and unified efforts. Characteristics of highly productive global project teams and traditional project teams are discussed in Chapters 5 and 6, respectively.

Going through the remaining chapters of the book, one may relate concepts, processes, and models presented in the book with project management experience to improve effectiveness as a member of the project team and as the project manager.

Questions:

1. Compare and contrast teams and groups.
2. How and why are project teams organized?
3. List some ways in which project managers can measure project team performance.
4. Relate project team development phases with the project life cycle. Are they project specific?
5. What traits and characteristics must be present for organizations to create successful project teams?

CHAPTER 2

Development of Project Teams

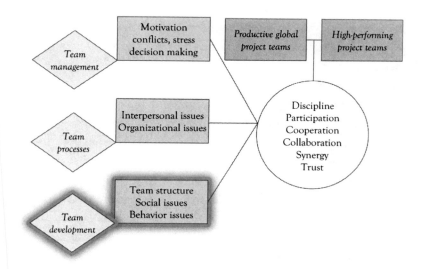

Objectives:

- Learn the social and psychological aspects of team development.
- Gain knowledge of different organization structures and their influence on the project team.
- Analyze the impact of culture on team performance.
- Explore generational differences and their influence on team communication.

Preview

The chapter begins by explaining the mind-sets behind team creation, and how to effectively motivate team members. This chapter succinctly advises that all situations are unique and that different techniques must be used to capitalize on the team's strengths. Type of organization structure presents strengths and weaknesses to project teams, and project managers must be aware and capitalize on their strengths. Project managers must structure their teams to fully utilize individual abilities, and to avoid possible obstacles to team effectiveness. The social and psychological aspects of team development are adequately captured in visual models and accompanying discussion. Another recurring topic that is introduced in this chapter is the impact of cultural and generational groups on team performance. Cultural differences are explained on a variety of spectrums; so future project managers can better understand and empathize with their diversified teams.

As is true with any team that is formed and developed to accomplish a mission or task in organizations, project teams are essential in planning and executing projects by harnessing efforts of multiple disciplines. Ideally, project teams aim to realize unified and collective effort and wisdom through harmony and the presence of a healthy conflict that promotes innovation. However, it is not an easy goal to accomplish in an ever-increasing diversity in workplace. As such, project teams are comprised of individuals with varying personality types, different skills and disciplines, experience, motivations, values, ethics, and attitudes. It is quite a challenge to develop effective and efficient project teams.

Motivation for Team Development

Motivation for a team's effectiveness and efficiency comes from two distinct and different approaches: task related and people related. The task-related approach focuses on the purpose for which the project team is selected, that is, to complete the project scope within the specified cost and time while satisfying customer and end-user needs. The people-related approach develops a cohesive team by addressing behavioral issues in a manner such that project goals are accomplished. In other words:

1. If one manages task-related issues such as scope, cost, and schedule issues properly, the people-related issues will be taken care of themselves.

2. If one manages the people-related issues properly, the project objectives or task-related issues such as cost/schedule/scope/quality will be taken care of themselves.

These motivational approaches also underline the importance of both project planning and team development. In other words, both the project planning and team development should occur as an integrated process for project success. Needless to say, both the task-related and people-related approaches are equally important in developing project teams. Depending on the situation at hand, the emphasis on one approach or the other or a combination of both the approaches is likely to lead to team success and provide desired results.

Research studies have identified several characteristics of a team that can help us identify attributes of team structures. These characteristics, their descriptions, and recommendations for teams are captured in Table 2.1.

The team characteristics listed in Table 2.1 have diverging importance in team structure for traditional teams and virtual teams. Of the characteristics listed in Table 2.1, task interdependence encourages project teams to work together collaboratively. Distributed leadership assumes importance for mega projects, whereas focused leadership and directive role of the project manager are of great importance for global projects, specifically during the initial phase of the project.

Different concepts are needed in selecting, structuring, and developing project teams for traditional and global projects. Traditional teams will have plenty of opportunities for social and informal interactions to understand individual and team roles and responsibilities, and to develop cohesion and collaboration among the team members. Global and virtual project teams, on the other hand, depend on technology for their formal interactions, which are mostly task focused. One cannot help but notice that the emphasis is exclusively on people-related issues.

Teams in an enterprise, from the perspective of task-related project management issues, such as scope, quality, cost, and time, can be broadly divided into four types: the proposal team, proposal portfolio team, project team, and project portfolio team. Their purpose and performance measures are shown in Table 2.2.

Table 2.1 Team structure: people related

Characteristics	Description	Discrete category
Task interdependence	The extent to which tasks and outcomes of individuals' tasks depend on actions of others	• Pooled—no direct interaction • Sequential—assembly-line type task relation • Reciprocal—one-on-one relation • Intensive—collaboration among all
Role structure	The extent to which • Roles are fundamentally different • Capable of performing independently	• Functional—distinct role, not interchangeable • Divisional—perform any piece of overall task
Leadership structure	The patters or distribution of leadership functions	• Focused—single leader • Distributed—two or more share leadership role
Communication structure	Flow of communication and information sharing among the team members	• Hub and wheel—flow through one person • Star—free flow among team members • Chain—hierarchical flow of information
Physical dispersion	Spatial location of team members with respect to others	• Colocated—physical proximity • Distributed—geographically dispersed • Mixed—subset of team colocated
Team duration	Time period of team's existence	• Ad hoc—specific task completion • Long term—unlimited number of tasks

Source: Adapted from Miloslavic, Wildman, and Thayer (2015); Wildman et al. (2012).

These four teams, with different success criteria, demand different team characteristics such as team structure, team size, team composition, and individual skills of team members. Nevertheless, team structure and team processes discussed in the chapter are relevant to a large extent for the entire project and proposal teams.

Project management literature and research have focused on task-related aspects from the beginning. It is possible that organizations can

Table 2.2 Team structure: task related

Team	Purpose	Success criteria
Proposal team	Responsible for drafting a compelling proposal for a forthcoming externally funded project	• Technical compatibility Staff capability New staff • Financial objectives Return on investment Risk involved in winning
Proposal portfolio team	Responsible for having the most relevant suite of proposals in the proposal pipeline	• Strategic objectives New market Market share • Financial objectives Win rate Payback/cash flow
Project team	Responsible for implementing the project's deliverable in line with its specifications for scope, cost, and time	• Cost • Time • Scope/quality
Project portfolio team	Responsible for having the most relevant suite of projects in the project pipeline	• Strategic alignment • Regulatory compliance

excel at achieving task-related project management issues by developing and applying sophisticated project management tools, techniques, procedures, and practices for requirement analysis and specifications, and development of scope, schedule, and cost of management plans. However, focus on people-related issues has been gaining importance in the last two decades and it presents greater challenges.

Furthermore, project planning for a specific project often involves work with no precedence or previous experience that one can refer to, whereas team development is an ongoing activity that can be continuously addressed and managed using the organization's team structures and processes to facilitate performance excellence. This chapter primarily emphasizes people-related issues in developing effective project teams.

Past studies on project management underline the value of a committed and effective project team, and presence of organizational processes and structures for making them effective and committed. The research has also highlighted the necessity to continue team building throughout the project, as project teams are transient.

Organization Structure and Its Impact on Project Teams

Organizational structure[1] is the sum total of the ways in which the organization divides its people into distinct tasks and then achieves coordination among them. In a similar vein, the project team structure represents a mechanism to assign project tasks to project team members and define interdependency among the task and team members to achieve collaborative and coordinated effort to meet project objectives.

The structure of the project team impacts performance and teamwork. Team structural characteristics include the number of team members, the status hierarchy, roles and responsibilities, and accepted norms for behaviors of the project team members. Some of these factors may vary based on the project size, complexity, and the context in which it operates, and its influence on team cohesion.

Project teams perform in organization structures that can be broadly classified as functional, projectized, and matrix structures. However, recent studies have added more variations to these three basis types of structures.

Functional Structure

In functional structures, each department maintains a strong concentration of technical or discipline-specific expertise. Since all projects must flow through the functional departments, each project can benefit from the most advanced knowledge, thereby making this organizational structure best suited for mass production. However, functional managers maintain absolute control over the budget; as they have flexibility with people and a broad base from which to work, many projects are likely to be completed within budget. Both the formal and informal organizations are well established and levels of authority and responsibility are clearly defined. Because each person reports to only one individual, communication channels are also structured well.

---

[1] Mintzberg (1979, 66).

One of the disadvantages is that there is no strong central authority or individual responsible for the total project. As a result, integration of activities that cross functional lines is difficult, and top-level executives must get involved in resolving conflict and making important decisions. Due to power struggles among various functional groups, functional managers tend to support what is best for their functional group or division rather than for the project. The decision-making process is slow and tedious, and many times, ideas will remain functionally oriented with little regard for ongoing projects.

Projectized Structure

In a functional structure, the projects are subordinate to divisional or functional managers. However, in projectized structure, divisions or functions are subordinate to projects.

A projectized structure (Table 2.3) is useful as long as there is a steady stream of projects, work is stable, and conflicts are at a minimum. The main advantage of this structure is that the project manager maintains complete line authority over the entire project. Furthermore, the project manager assigns work and conducts performance reviews. Strong communication channels can be developed that would result in rapid response time.

Table 2.3 Projectized organization

Advantages	Disadvantages
Project manager has the authority	The structure might cause replication of efforts
Team members report to the project manager	Team members may be retained after the project is complete
Structure provides strong communication channels	Discipline-specific competency suffers
Opportunity to maintain expertise on a given project	Lack of opportunity for interaction with functional groups
Decision-making process could be efficient	Lack of professional growth for project team

Source: Adapted from Kerzner (2009).

The major disadvantage is the cost of maintaining the organizational structure. Individuals cannot be shared with another project to reduce costs. Personnel then are attached to their projects longer than they are needed because once an employee is given up, the project manager may not be able to get the employee back. At project completion, people do not have a home to return to in the organization. Motivating people is another problem. Equipment and facilities also present concerns and conflicts.

Matrix Structure

The matrix structure is a blend of both functional and projectized structures to varying degrees and the relation between projects and divisions would depend on the dominance or balance of projectized and functional structures. Therefore, the matrix structure can be better or worse in comparison to the other two structures.

Obviously, the matrix structure is the most complex of all organizational forms. Careful consideration must be given to where and how the organization fits in the total organization. Consider the matrix where complex, short-run projects are the organization's primary output; when a complicated design calls for both innovation and timely completion; where several sophisticated skills are needed; and when there is a rapidly changing marketplace.

No one has a single organizational authority—and yet it works (Table 2.4). There is dual accountability. The project environment and the functional environment cannot be separated; they must interact. Individuals must take direction from both the project manager and the functional manager. Performance reviews generally remain with the functional manager.

Similar to democracy being considered the worst form of government and yet being better than anything else, many consider the matrix organization better than other forms or organization structures. Research results and opinions vary as to which is the best organizational structure for project teams to perform optimally. Under conditions of high uncertainty, a more decentralized structure such as project matrix or projectized structure is preferred and the project team (projectized structure) is the most

Table 2.4 Matrix organization

Advantages	Disadvantages
Project manager has maximum project control	Multidimensional information flow
Policies and procedures can be set up for each project separately	Dual reporting
Project manager has authority to commit resources	Continuously changing priorities
Rapid response to changes, conflicts, and project needs	Management goals are different from project goals
Each team member has "home" after project completion	Balance of time, cost, and performance must be monitored

Source: Adapted from Kerzner (2009).

effective, followed by project matrix and the functional organization is considered least effective.[2] Obviously, a projectized structure is the most preferred organization structure because projects are often associated with uncertainty and unknowns. Project managers seeking efficient use of resources and benefit from inter-project cooperation prefer functional matrix.[3]

Individual Roles in Project Teams

Often project teams present different values and expectations of behaviors to complete assigned project tasks. Individual roles—that of a leader, planner, communicator, scheduler, executioner, coordinator, risk analyst, and the like—should be assigned based on strengths of individuals. Personality types and individual strengths such as attention to details, ability to see the big picture, need for success, and fear of failure help us to assign team roles. Individuals can assume more than one role but workload balance is necessary and one has to be careful in avoiding conflicting roles. All the while, it is good to remember that individual roles and responsibilities are assigned for the purpose of meeting project objectives and outcomes successfully.

---

[2] Hyväri (2006).
[3] Laslo and Golberg (2008).

It is important to define roles and responsibilities of project team members without ambiguity as it would encourage teamwork and reduce conflict. Clear assignments of roles and responsibilities without ambiguity or overlapping responsibilities are important for avoiding conflicts, conflict resolution, and achieving productivity gains. Matching skills and expertise with roles and responsibilities would lead to effective use of project team members and their expertise. It also helps functional managers to understand the project requirements and provide support. Clear definition of roles and responsibilities will also help in establishing an environment of trust among the project team members. A research study[4] showed that defining project processes and roles is the first and most important step for managing and leading project teams and projects successfully.

With a primary focus on hard project-management tools and techniques to meet project goals such as schedule, budget, and scope, which is often the case, it is likely that the project manager may lose the sight of a more subjective aspect of managing projects—the team member. Each person brings a unique set of experiences and knowledge to the project team. Equally important are the social and behavioral skills that each individual uses to interact with other team members in forming a cohesive and productive team. A project manager may spend significant effort and funds on team building, only to find that his team still does not reach its full potential due to one or more team members who, either consciously or unconsciously, do not integrate with the team.[5] Ultimately, one must remember that project team members must handle people issues well, while crafting/managing the technical issues and project outcomes skillfully.

Social and Behavioral Issues of Teams

Social psychology consents that people have the propensity to categorize other people and things into either *same* or *different*.[6] Furthermore,

---

[4] Anantatmula (2008).
[5] Adams and Anantatmula (2010).
[6] Wildman and Griffith (2015).

our innate tendency to interpret unfamiliarity (*difference*) as a threat may affect collaboration as unfamiliarity leads to a chain reaction of undesirable attitudes and behaviors. This is an important challenge in managing teams, specifically global project teams, where diversity and cultural differences assume importance in team learning and effectiveness.

The idea of the *same and difference concept* is prevalent in many aspects of our lives. We look for and align with people of similar age group, same language, same geographical location, similar profession, fans of sports teams, and so on. It is a natural phenomenon and we are generally more comfortable with familiarity and tend to be on a quest for familiarity in unfamiliar situations and places. With many languages, customs, and diverse cultures, Indians demonstrate the *same and difference concept* in India and abroad by forming associations and networks based on language and region.

When you are in a country that speaks a different language and when you are noticed as a foreign person, by speaking a word or two in their native language could bring a smile and warm response to your question or greeting.

As a project manager, one should recognize and address unfamiliar issues during the initial stages of team development. By identifying and nurturing the *same* aspect among the team members, project managers can speed up the process of team cohesion and coordination. Needless to say, understanding the social and behavioral skills that each individual employs is critical in developing a productive team. During the forming or initial stages of team, individuals do not instantly become cohesive and unified. Each person's personal history dictates one's self-perceptions and exhibited behaviors in social settings. Individuals use these learned behaviors to influence others and to be influenced as well. As teams mature, the emotional reactions of team members tend to synchronize eventually.

The project manager must recognize and appreciate the individual's social and behavioral journey to develop effective teams. It starts with the development of a unique self-identity and ends with full team integration in a state of emotional intelligence (Figure 2.1).

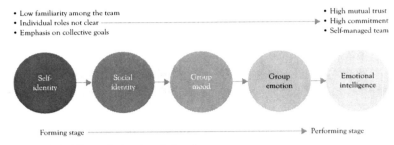

- Low familiarity among the team
- Individual roles not clear
- Emphasis on collective goals

- High mutual trust
- High commitment
- Self-managed team

Self-identity → Social identity → Group mood → Group emotion → Emotional intelligence

Forming stage ————————————————————————— ▶ Performing stage

Figure 2.1 Team behavioral development process

Table 2.5 Team structure and characteristics

Characteristics	Description
Self-identity	Self-identity is a person's way of defining who he or she is as a unique individual in relationship to the rest of the world.
Social identity	Social identity is developed from interactions with a team, wherein both individuals and the team influence each other.
Group emotion	Personal emotions can be elevated to a group level to become group emotion. Individuals may perceive the group emotions as being larger and more important than their individual emotions.
Group mood	Group mood is a natural extension of group emotion. Emotions are temporary, quick, and reactive, whereas moods last for an extended period of time.
Emotional intelligence	Emotional intelligence is a state in which individuals learn not only to observe and to mimic but also to harness and control the team's emotions to aid in their thought processes. Complete trust is established at this stage.

Self-identity of a person and the development of social skills begin at birth with family interactions (Table 2.5). The individual strives to learn acceptable social skills, which are unique to his family structure, ethnic culture, and socioeconomic situation. In addition to family influences, an individual's innate needs can influence his interactions with the team. They are the need for affiliation and the need for achievement. Furthermore, birth order within the family can also predict need tendencies and how much effort an individual will expend to fit into a team. However, as part of a group in adulthood, one may unconsciously revert to the role held within the family group, if group norms are at odds with the self-identity.

Social identity is the process of deriving one's self-perceptions from an affiliation with a group. An individual, who is associated with a strong and positive group, would internalize the positive attributes of the group as part of his self-identity. However, if the group with which the individual affiliates is weak or has negative attributes, the individual will disassociate from the group and will revert to one's previous self-identity. Furthermore, team factors outside of an individual's control, such as being a member of a minority group, can also influence social identity. Prior relationships between team members, such as acquaintances and friends, can predict team success and team member satisfaction with the team process. Although the team influences the individual, research studies prove that the individual can also consciously modify verbal and nonverbal behaviors in social settings to influence the team. This two-way exchange begins the real process of team building and cohesion.

Group emotion: Personal emotions can be elevated to a group level to transform into group emotion. Positive emotions—such as happiness and compassion—will lead to group closeness and bind the group together. Negative emotions, such as anger and jealousy, will increase anxiety and fear and lead to a desire for avoidance and a disassociation from the group identity. Individuals may perceive the group emotion as being larger and more important than their individual emotions. This sense of shared importance can inspire an individual to take action on behalf of the group that, otherwise, would not be attempted by the individual. Positive group emotions often lead to beneficial results for teams. As a leader, one must display positive emotion not only to influence others in the team but also to elevate one's status in the team.

Group mood is a natural extension of group emotion that moves teams to the next level. Emotions are temporary, quick, and reactive, whereas moods last for an extended period of time. As an established member of a team, an individual will, over time, detect subtle changes in nonverbal expressions, gestures, or speech of other team members. When a team works together for a period of time, the individual learns to interpret expressions of fellow team members and associates them with feelings or emotions. The individual will then unconsciously mimic expressions in an effort to maintain his or her status within the team. As team members continue to develop and mimic this awareness of each other, the team develops a group mood. Verbal and nonverbal cues are emphasized, recognized, and acted upon similarly by each team member. When teams reach a state of group mood, the members surpass the temporary and fleeting state of emotions. As the team member unconsciously synchronizes self and social behaviors with those of teammates, the focus shifts from the self to the team. At this stage in the team process life cycle, team cohesion is fully functional.

Emotional intelligence: As teams continue to mature, group mood can be elevated even further to the level of emotional intelligence. When a team reaches a state of emotional intelligence, individuals learn not only to observe and mimic but also to harness and control the team's emotions to influence their thought processes. In this elevated social state, the team, feeling safety and trust among the members, is comfortable in setting standards on positive and negative behaviors. Also, the team as a unit will react to emotional stress easily. The focus of the team is turned back to the individual's perspective, interpreting and reacting to the individual's behaviors while maintaining emotional balance. A team that is able to achieve this level becomes self-managed and highly productive. Team members work more efficiently together as a group than as individuals while being acutely aware of individual needs.

Emotional intelligence is considered as the ability to perceive emotions, to access and generate emotions so as to assist thought, to understand emotions and emotional knowledge, and to reflectively regulate emotions so as to promote emotional and intellectual growth.[7] In other words, *emotional intelligence* encompasses your ability to recognize how you and those around you are feeling, ability to generate emotion, and then reason with this emotion, ability to understand complex emotions and how emotions transition from one stage to another, and the ability to manage emotions in yourself and in others.

Importance of emotional intelligence for teams: Often perceived as an individual competency, emotional intelligence is necessary for project teams to improve performance and success. Three essential conditions are identified for a group's effectiveness:[8] trust among members, a sense of

---

[7] Mayer and Salovey (1997).
[8] Druskat and Wolff (2001).

Table 2.6 Emotional intelligence team

Team members are aware of other individual team members' emotions and are adept at regulating them
Team members do not hesitate to confront one another if norms are broken
Demonstrate a high level of self-awareness by seeking feedback from within and outside the team
Work very closely with clients and customers
Aware of the needs and concerns of people outside the team and use them to develop relations
Solve problems proactively
Create resources and allocate time to work with emotions and related issues

Source: Druskat and Wolff (2001).

group identity, and a sense of group efficacy. Due to multiple interactions at different levels, team emotional intelligence is considered more intricate than individual emotional intelligence. Individual emotional intelligence focus is inward whereas a group emotional intelligence is outward, as one must pay attention to emotions of all the members of the group. Characteristics of a model emotional intelligence team are presented in Table 2.6.

In addition to the presence of characteristics listed in Table 2.6, project goals and project deliverables require a unified and collaborative effort from the project team and, consequently, a common commitment is natural to many project teams. Together, all these attributes lead to a self-managed and productive team.

Cultural Issues and Influence on Teams

Depending on the context, the word "culture" assumes different meanings. In the context of teams, culture denotes organizational behavior, social behavior, practices, beliefs, work ethics, and values of team members.

Managing cultural differences is challenging and if not managed well, teams will be dysfunctional. The corporate workforce is becoming increasingly dispersed and diverse, thereby posing challenges to sustain and promote organization culture. Several past studies identified culture as a cause of project failure. Specifically, global projects will have to deal with multiple cultures, and the role of culture in project performance assumes greater importance. The project manager needs to be aware of and understand how culture can and will impact the project performance.

It is common knowledge that culture begins in the family for generations to help create our values, perceptions, customs, and behaviors. For this reason, culture could be different within the same geographical region. Differences in race, religion, gender, and even age can create cultural differences, and such differences can be found within the family and among neighbors. A frequent discussion topic is the communication and cultural gap between Gen Y and Baby Boomers and the importance of addressing it in workplace. From this perspective, culture is defined as the behaviors and beliefs characteristic of a particular social, ethnic, or age group. From project management perspective, there is concern about the work culture of an organization. The larger context and its culture are relevant, however. Various definitions of culture are presented in Table 2.7.

An *organization culture* (*work culture*) is shared beliefs, values, and practices of individuals or groups in an organization that influence norms

Table 2.7 Definitions of culture

Definition	Source
Shared motives, values, beliefs, identities, and interpretations or meanings of significant events that (cultures) result from common experiences of members of collectivities that are transmitted across generations.	Gabrenya and Smith (2015) citing the Global Leadership and Organizational Behavioral Effectiveness project's definition.
"The collective programming of the mind which distinguishes the members of one group or category of people from another."	Hofstede (1997, 5)
"... the shared ways groups of people understand and interpret the world."	Trompenaars and Hampden-Turner (1998, 3)
The culture of a group is a set of shared basic assumptions based on learning by solving problems that proved to be valid over time and therefore, passed on to new members as the correct way to perceive, think, and feel in relation to those problems.	Schein (1993)
National culture is broadly defined as values, beliefs, norms, and behavioral patterns of a national group.	Hofstede (1980)

and behavior of both individuals and groups of that organization. Development of an organizational culture is usually a slow process and, once developed, it is equally slow to change.

Shared values, beliefs, and behavioral norms assume importance at an individual level, whereas shared work practices, shared work ethics, processes, and work norms assume importance at the organizational level. Of these work culture elements, processes can be more easily manipulated to influence the work culture.

It is typical to stereotype people's behavior, work ethics, and other work-related traits based on their native country and, to some extent, based on their geographical region if one is not knowledgeable about that specific country or region. In reality, the issue is more complex and culture varies with every nation in a geographic region such as Pacific Asia and Southeast Asia. Furthermore, one can observe subtle variances among regions within a nation such as South India and North India or Texas and California. There are even subtle differences among various states and among different regions within a nation, not to mention that every individual is different (Figure 2.2).

As can be seen from Figure 2.2, an individual's culture has several layers of influence. Furthermore, differences among individuals and culture impact interactions among people. So, how realistic are the stereotype assumptions that are often made about an individual, a nation, and a region?

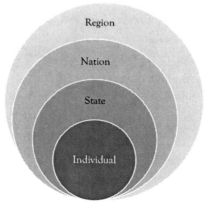

Figure 2.2 Culture—levels of difference among people

Figure 2.3 Culture—levels of difference based on association

There is a need to appreciate cultural differences and individual differences to work well in diverse teams. These differences are wrapped up with differences among professional practices, organizations, industries, and regions,[9] and these invisible boundaries divide our world (Figure 2.3). The commonality reduces as you move from the inner circle to the outer circle.

Success in this global economy largely depends on how one navigates through drastically different cultural realities. If not managed well, these cultural variances could lead to failures due to major communication gaps and misunderstandings. It is apt for project teams that manage global projects and virtual teams.

An additional layer of complexity in dealing with multiple cultures is *ethnocentrism*. Individuals often fall into the trap of *ethnocentrism*,[10] "the tendency for people to evaluate a foreigner's behavior by the standards of their own culture, which they believe is superior to all others." Although *ethnocentrism* can strengthen unity among groups with similar beliefs and cultural values, it can derail relations with people from other cultures. Managers must be aware of this tendency and make a conscious effort to recognize, understand, and address cultural differences in a cross-cultural work environment that is present in traditional projects, and specifically

[9] Meyer (2014).
[10] Ferraro and Briody (2013, 22).

in international and global projects in which people from different countries work together toward a common project goal.

High-Context and Low-Context Cultures

An interesting and important research study has classified national cultures as high context and low context.[11] In a *high-context* culture, contextual elements help people to understand the rules. One cannot take the literary meaning of what people from the high-context cultures say. You need to understand what is unspoken and what the unwritten rules are. Countries with a long history and traditions such as China, India, Japan, France, Germany, Spain, and France fall into this category. In a *low-context culture*, what you say is what you mean; there are no hidden messages and the chances of misunderstanding are less among people who belong to this culture. Countries like the United States, Canada, Australia, and Netherlands fall into this category (Table 2.8).

Table 2.8 High-context and low-context cultures

Factor	High-context culture	Low-context culture
Openness of message	Covert and implicit message	Explicit, simple' and clear message
Attribution for failure	Personal acceptance	Blame others
Nonverbal communication	High	Low
Expression of reaction	Reserved and inward	Visible and outward
Cohesion and groups	Distinction of in-group and out-group. Strong sense of family	Flexible and open groups. Changing as needed
Bonding with people	Strong bonds with affinity to family and community	Fragile bonding with people with little sense of loyalty
Commitment to relations	High commitment to relationships. Relationships over tasks	Low commitment to relationships. Tasks over relationships
Flexibility with time	Open and flexible. Process over product	Organized and inflexible. Product over process

---

[11] Hall (1984).

One will find that contracts in France tend to be short and much of the information is drawn from the high-context culture. In the United States, contracts are written elaborately by taking into account each and every issue in detail and every possible scenario.

When managing a global project team of diverse cultures representing heterogeneity, it is safe to adapt low-context culture to avoid miscommunication. However, when managing a project team that is colocated and culturally homogeneous, you can adopt the resident culture that could be either high or low context.

Cultural Dimensions

The Global Leadership and Organizational Leadership Behavior Effectiveness (GLOBE) project, managed by a large group of psychologists and faculty, expanded Hofstede's original definition of dimensions (Table 2.9).

Erin Meyer (2014) proposes an eight-scale model of cultural spectrum of one extreme to the other mentioned as follows:

1. *Communicating*: low context versus high context
2. *Evaluating*: direct negative feedback versus indirect negative feedback
3. *Persuading*: principles first versus applications first
4. *Leading*: egalitarian versus hierarchical

Table 2.9 GLOBE's definition of culture

Uncertainty avoidance: reliance on rules and norms to alleviate unpredictability
Power distance: expectation for power to be distributed unequally
Individualism and collectivism: organization and society encourage collective action (institutional collectivism); individuals are loyal to organizations and families (in-group collectivism)
Gender egalitarianism: collectively minimized gender equality
Future orientation: individuals delay gratification, plan, and invest in future
Performance orientation: performance improvement and excellence is encouraged and rewarded
Humane orientation: individuals are rewarded for being fair, altruistic, generous, caring, and kind

5. *Deciding*: consensual versus top-down
6. *Trusting*: task based versus relationship based
7. *Disagreeing*: confrontational versus avoids confrontation
8. *Scheduling*: linear time versus flexible time

Culture sets the range on the two extreme points of the scale for each of these eight dimensions, and an individual takes a position within that range. Another important aspect of these eight scales is how people from different cultures relate to one another, not with an absolute position but with a relative position of two cultures. For instance, the way Japanese people are perceived by India and the United States is different because of their relative positions on each of these eight scales. You may find similar differences within different regions of a country as well.

The language of a society and its history influence the communication style that might fall within the range of either explicit or implicit communication styles. People in the United States communicate explicitly, that is, characterized with low-context messages, whereas people from some of the ancient societies such as Spain, India, and Japan communicate implicitly, and messages are to be understood in context. Table 2.10 illustrates this aspect effectively.

Table 2.10 Influence of context in communication

What the British say	What the British mean	What the Dutch understand
I hear what you say	I disagree completely	He accepts my point of view
Very interesting	I do not agree	He likes my idea
I almost agree	I do not agree	He almost agrees
I am sure it is my fault	It is not my fault	It is his fault
This is an original point of view	You must be crazy	They like the idea
With the greatest respect	You must be a fool	He respects me/my view
I would suggest	Do it as I want to	An open suggestion
Not bad	(Very) good	Average or poor
By the way	The primary purpose is	Not very important

Source: Adapted from Rottier, Ripmeester, and Bush (2011).

Culture and Communications

These cultural differences underline the importance of nonverbal communication and listening skills. Specifically, both play a key role when you communicate with a person from a different culture. To be an effective communicator or a successful project team leader in this global economy of diverse cultures and many languages, it is a good idea to learn about the context culture and how the message will be perceived. It is worth investing your time and effort in understanding cultural differences and communication styles when dealing with people from different countries. In some cases, as Erin Meyer points out, it is a good idea to build relations first.

A cardinal rule in communications is to ensure that the message is received as intended. Sometimes, one need not be candid if it adversely impacts the delivery and content of the message. It is not important what is said or how one acts; what matters the most is how others perceive your message. It becomes necessary to adjust the message content and delivery style in line with the culture and context of the receiver of the communication.

Culture and Time: Scheduling Challenges for Projects

Each of us is bound by time. Unquestionably, projects are also time bound. In the context of people adhering to schedules and punctuality, time aspect of cultural differences among countries and regions prompted in defining monochromic time (M-time) and polychromic time (P-time).[12]

M-time is about doing one thing at a time and requires careful planning and scheduling. Industrialized societies adapted to this time scale. For them, time is specific and real. People, who are accustomed to M-time, allow the time to control their lives. These individuals prefer to be on time for meetings and make their best effort to complete their work on time.

In P-time culture, human interactions and relations are valued over time and materialistic things. Work gets done at one's own pace, which is often unpredictable. People may not take appointments seriously and

---

[12] Hall (1984).

Table 2.11 Scheduling challenges

Factor	M-time action	P-time action
Actions	Do one thing at a time	Do many things at once
Focus	Concentrate on the job at hand	Easily distracted from work
Attention to time	When things must be achieved	What will be achieved
Priority	Put the job first	Put relations first
Respect for property	Seldom borrow or lend things	Borrow and lend things often and easily
Timeliness	Emphasize promptness	Base promptness on relationship factors

often come late. When managing a team of diverse people from different cultures, you need to understand the cultural differences of M-time and P-time (Table 2.11).

These differences would impact meetings, appointments, the value that you assign to your time, and daily work schedule, not to mention the project schedule being managed.

In M-time culture, meetings start on time, have a set agenda, and end at a preset time. If there is an attempt to hijack the meeting discussion in a tangential direction, the facilitator takes the responsibility of bringing it back to the issue at hand. Otherwise, the rest of the attendees may not cooperate with the initiator.

In P-time culture, meetings take impulsive directions with no attention to time. When managing the meeting in this culture, one needs to be adaptable and professional to get desired outcomes from these discussions and realize the meeting goals. One needs to be flexible with an open mind and should be an opportunist to steer the meeting in the right direction.

When managing projects, it is preferable to train and realign all the team members to M-time. The best way is to let the team participate in developing a team charter. This will be discussed later.

Culture and Trust

Trust is classified into affective trust and cognitive trust. Affective trust is based on relations in the workplace and is based on emotional closeness, empathy, or friendship. If trust is based on feeling comfortable and confident about a person based on accomplishments, skills, and reliability comprised of consistency and transparency, it is cognitive trust. These two trusts denote task-based and relation-based cultures respectively.

An environment of trust is influenced by the organizational culture that promotes transparency, collaboration, and openness. It ultimately leads to a cohesive project team.

Generational Bias

Generational differences and their consequences are rarely considered or discussed in the context of projects and project teams. More often than not, the current reality is that people from four generations work together in project teams and their work-related differences deserve attention. Given the importance of projects, it is critical that organizations engage people from different generations productively to complete projects.

The term generation is defined as an identifiable group that shares years of birth, location, and significant life events at critical stages of development.[13] Different studies identified different time periods and characteristics. While differences exist among studies in the precise years of birth that define the different generations, it is generally agreed that there are four generations. These four generations, ranging from oldest to youngest, are the Veterans, Baby Boomers, Generation X, and Generation Y. Furthermore, the past research findings suggest that both similarities and differences exist among all these four groups (Table 2.12).

Veterans prefer job security and are loyal to organizations. They have a good work ethic and show respect to their leaders. Veterans are formal in their attire and use formal style of communication.

Baby Boomers are considered optimistic, team oriented, and willing to go the extra mile. They tend to have great communication skills in impacting organizational change and building consensus. Baby Boomers are often looked upon as mentors in the organization because of their interpersonal skills. However, they are often considered as workaholics and competitive.

---

[13] Kupperschmidt (2000).

Table 2.12 Generations at work

Factor	Veterans	Baby Boomers	Generation X	Generation Y
Time period	1922–1945	1946–1964	1965–1979	1980–2001
Generation	Traditionals Matures Silent generation GI generation	Boomers	Post Boomers Baby Busters	Millennials Nexters Me generation
Workplace traits	Strong work ethic Respect authority	Team oriented Optimistic Value relationships Sacrifice Loyal Work hard	Practical Pessimistic Maintain work–life balance Technical Independent Adaptable	Ambitious Maintain self-esteem Narcissistic Technical Independent Multitasking
Leadership style	Military chain of command	Influencing Having high expectations Mentoring	Practical Goal oriented	Flexible Adaptable Lack social grace Ambitious
Motivation	Value of experience Value of loyalty Value of perseverance	Demonstration of their ability Bonus and other incentives Value of their contribution	Work–life balance non-hierarchical structure Time-off as incentive Loyalty	Higher position Monetary gains Lower need for social approval Innovation
Learning style	Classroom On-the-job training	Classroom instructor focused	Technology focus Mentors	Creative thinking Visual

Source: Adapted from Anantatmula and Shrivastav (2012).

Generation X people invest their efforts for their growth rather than their employers. They are highly adaptable to technology. Generation X people bring a realistic and practical approach to solving problems. They prefer working in organizations that are not very hierarchical in structure and are eager to add value.

Generation Y people are ethnically diverse, global, independent, confident, and adaptive to various situations and multitasking. They often lack loyalty toward their employers, and are prone to taking risks, and may easily switch to other jobs. Members of Generation Y demonstrate higher self-esteem, personal admiration, anxiety, depression, and lower need for social approval. They are technically savvy.

Research has shown that the generation gap is an issue and it is more significant between Generation Y and Baby Boomers.[14] The research observed that Generation Y has fewer issues in dealing with Generation X. Specifically, Generation Y is viewed unfavorably and struggles in the workplace due to differences arising out of the generation gap.

Many generation-specific attributes—work values; traits and attitudes; preferences in workplace; communication styles; and attitude toward technology, leadership style, and motivation—will have an impact on multigenerational teams. For example, technology and preferences for the medium of communication are distinctly different for each generation. Specifically, Generation Y focuses on e-mailing or on texting while the other generations prefer phone or face-to-face interaction. Generation Y people are visual learners compared to other generations because they have had exposure or owned a computer at a young age, have had experience utilizing the Internet, and can retrieve any information from the vast and often intriguing sources of information on the Internet. Generation Y preference in using technology extends to the workplace. Thus, from a project manager's perspective, the use of technology would entice the Generation Y to communicate, and to participate more actively.

In project management, the skills for working together are of very great importance. Therefore, project managers must be open to the concerns of Generation Y, as they learn the organizational culture, and as they improve their domain-specific knowledge. Assigning a mentor to assist the Generation Y in bridging the knowledge gap assumes importance in developing and managing project teams. Lastly, project managers need to address the potential issues associated with generational differences as part of the project charter, and the subsequent kickoff meeting. Clearly defining roles and honing people skills, inclusion, and recognition for younger generations would help in improving team cohesion.

When project managers start customizing the project tasks and goals for the project team by defining roles and responsibilities, it would be

---

[14] Anantatmula and Shrivastav (2012).

helpful to allow everyone to participate in the process. Involving Generation Y in decision making and aligning their professional goals with the project goals would lead to greater commitment to the project, and to the organization as well. It is desirable to incorporate participation, inclusion, and recognition throughout the project management life cycle, but more specifically in the project closeout phase in which lessons learned are captured and important achievements of the project are celebrated.

Questions:

1. Discuss different motivational techniques.
2. List the various characteristics of a team.
3. Explain how project teams interact to complete projects.
4. Give examples where the different organization structural approaches are appropriate.
5. Show how individual characteristics have an impact on team structure.
6. Explore behavioral issues and their impact on project performance.
7. Examine how generational differences in project teams have their impact on project performance.

CHAPTER 3

Project Team Processes

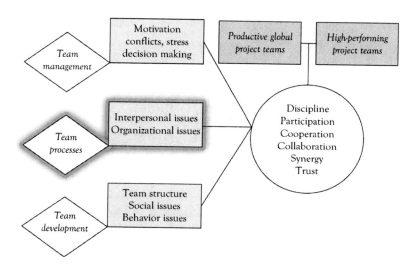

Objectives:

- Understand the team-development processes.
- Recognize processes to improve project team performance.
- Learn the characteristics required of successful leaders.
- Apply different team-development processes to various business situations and projects.
- Explore the value of lessons learned and develop appropriate strategies for capturing lessons learned.

Preview

This chapter focuses on the next aspect of teamwork: the actual processes that teams undergo for their effective performance. The discussion clearly differentiates processes and projects, noting the necessity of both. Various team development processes are explained with discussions and using the process models. The focus is on what is required by capable project leaders, and what different factors will impact their leadership ability. Communication and similar interpersonal skills are extensively discussed to underscore the possible cause–effect relationships that can stem from interpersonal situations. The chapter also underscores the importance of technology tools in managing projects. Many theoretical aspects of leadership and performance management are explained using examples, and their close relationship with knowledge management (KM) and learning are discussed in detail.

A team can perform effectively and efficiently when proven and established processes are in place. This is particularly important for project teams so that they can focus primarily on the uncertainties and unknowns of the project and not on redefining processes associated with team development and performance.

A process is defined as a group of repetitive and related actions that are systematic to achieve a specific result or service or end. A process is usually designed to improve productivity. Therefore, processes can be changed and revised when there is a need to improve efficiency and effectiveness.

Processes are ongoing, repetitive, and produce the same result, whereas projects are temporary and unique, and project outcomes are essentially new. However, processes are integral to projects, project teams, and project management (PM). Just like projects go through various task-related project management processes such as planning, executing, monitoring and controlling, and closing processes, the project team goes through similar processes such as team selection, team development, team performance, and termination. Furthermore, individual phases of team processes like team development and team performance can have multiple subprocesses. Some of these processes are standard and explicitly defined; a few others may have to be adapted to specific project situations.

Team Process and Taskwork

A team process is characterized by members interacting with other members and with their task environment. It is a mediating mechanism linking variables such as team members and organizational characteristics including structure, culture, supporting systems, performance and incentive systems, employee morale, and top management support.

Team processes are used to direct, align, and monitor *taskwork*, which are mostly people-related activities of coordination, communication, collaboration, decision making, and conflict management.

Taskwork, in the context of projects, is comprised of task-related activities such as project plan, requirement analysis, scope definition and development, project schedule, project budget, project execution, quality management, and monitoring and control.

A distinction between team processes and *taskwork* is that the latter is defined as *a team's interactions with tasks, tools, machines, and systems.*[1] *Taskwork* represents *what* it is that teams are doing, whereas team process describes *how* work is being accomplished.

Taskwork is critical to team effectiveness and depends heavily on member competence and *team processes.* Together, *taskwork* and *team processes* would determine a team's effectiveness and efficiency.

Team-Development Process

Classic theories suggest that teams develop through a series of four stages: forming, norming, storming, and performing.[2] These four stages of team development are seen as a linear progression. This may not always be true and new theories are emerging. However, it is helpful to present this classic team-development process to provide a basis for discussion on team development.

As one moves from the forming stage toward the performing stage, team performance and productivity are likely to improve. The four-stage team development model combines both task-related and people-related activities (Figure 3.1).

Forming stage: When team members first come together, as a first step toward becoming an integrated and cohesive unit, the project manager must help them become acquainted with one another. Team members will have many questions such as who are the other members, what is

---

[1] Bowers, Braun, and Morgan (1997, 90).
[2] Tuckman (1965).

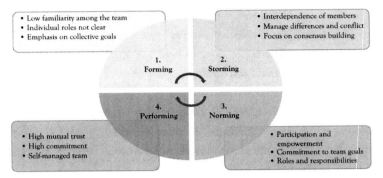

Figure 3.1 Team-development process

expected of them, and who is leading. The project manager needs to provide direction during this stage and curb negative emotions.

Storming stage: At this stage, team members are likely to explore different roles, understand dependencies, and express their differences. These behaviors often lead to conflict and counterdependence. The long-term success of the team depends on its ability to successfully overcome these problems. The typical interpersonal behaviors that signal this stage are the formation of coalitions, competition among members, disagreement with the leader, and challenges to one another's points of view. Fostering win–win relationships is critical.

Norming stage: After team members become acquainted with one another, the next stage of team development involves creating a sense of team identity and unity, which can be accelerated by additional means such as informal social gatherings. During this stage, the primary focus is on defining processes for a coordinated effort to execute project work, defining roles and responsibilities of the team, communicating expectations, and developing a work culture of working together.

Performing stage: Teams realize the need for collaboration, continuous improvement, and productivity. The team tends to become more effective and efficient, with an emphasis on quality. Strengthening relationships, commitment, support, and learning are emphasized as teams share vision and develop trust. The project manager needs to provide a supportive leadership role.

It is not necessary that every project team go through these four stages sequentially. Factors such as the project size, project team size, urgency, and complexity would influence the duration and sequence of these stages, which may overlap. Furthermore, the nature of the project team (traditional or virtual) would also influence these four stages.

Project Team Process

The team-development process can also be viewed as three action phases.[3] (Figure 3.2).

Project teams start with the *transition processes,* in which team members set goals and develop plans to meet these goals through analysis by obtaining requirements, developing specifications, defining scope, and developing comprehensive project plan, in that order.

As *transition processes* are evolving, *action processes* such as project execution, monitoring, and controlling will overlap with the final stages of the *transition processes.* During the *action processes,* team members coordinate, monitor progress, and develop change plans if necessary.

Interpersonal processes take place throughout the transition and action processes and people-related activities such as team selection and development, definition of roles and responsibilities, communication, collaboration, conflict management, and motivation are addressed.

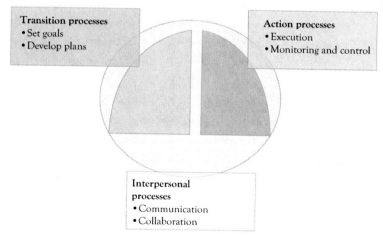

Transition processes
• Set goals
• Develop plans

Action processes
• Execution
• Monitoring and control

Interpersonal processes
• Communication
• Collaboration

Figure 3.2 Team process

---

[3] Marks, Mathieu, and Zaccaro (2001).

In other words, *transition processes* and *action processes* are *task-related processes* and *interpersonal processes* are people-related processes.

Emergent states describe the cognitive, motivational, and affective states of teams, as opposed to the nature of their member interactions.[4] Teams with low cohesion (an emergent state) may be less willing to manage existing conflict (the process), which, in turn, may create an additional conflict that lowers cohesion levels even further. Emergent states do not represent team interaction or team actions that lead toward outcomes. Rather, they are products of team experiences (including team processes) and become new inputs to subsequent processes and outcomes.

Team Management and Leadership Process

Of all the resources, managing human resources presents more challenges. Managing and leading people are the most challenging aspects of managing a team and deserve special attention and a clearly defined process is justified, specifically in projects.

It is important to understand the distinction between management and leadership, which is not always obvious. Management is usually focused on classical functions such as planning, organizing, and controlling. In general, management is concerned with making decisions about processes and functions in order to improve operational efficiency and effectiveness. Leadership, on the other hand, is about motivating and guiding people to realize their potential and achieve tougher and challenging organizational goals.

Projects, by definition, are new and unique. Consequently, they have little precedence and are often associated with uncertainties and unknowns. It is reasonable to assume that it is not if the project plan will change, but when the change occurs, what the change will be, and by how much. Furthermore, the absence of control over project team selection and lack of formal authority over project team members contribute to the challenges associated with managing and leading a project.

Project teams are comprised of people from multiple disciplines, as project tasks require expertise and skills in several disciplines.

---

[4] Marks, Mathieu, and Zaccaro (2001).

Furthermore, project tasks are characterized by risks, unknowns, and uncertainties. Consequently, projects often have to deal with changes. In general, projects also have to deal with complexity. Furthermore, time and budget constraints, uncertainties, and unknowns contribute to project complexity. The complexity demands that project managers plan and manage projects within the competing constraints of scope (project outcomes), cost, and duration. It is not always possible to meet the goals of one of them without compromising other two constraints. Priority would be given to the one that is more important for the client.

Several project characteristics underscore the importance of management and leadership roles in project performance. When projects are complex, the project manager's emphasis will be on the management role of planning and controlling. When changes are significant, the leadership role assumes greater importance. Leadership then is directed toward convincing people about the need to change, aligning them to a new direction, and motivating people to work together to achieve project objectives under difficult and demanding work environments.

While project-related factors such as complexity, uncertainty, unknowns, and risk may vary for each project, people- and team-related management and leadership roles and the responsibilities of the project manager, to a great extent, are common and similar in all the projects. After a comprehensive study of past research and a survey of several project management professionals, people-related project performance factors are identified (Table 3.1) and their interdependencies (arrow means "leads to") are shown as the team leadership process (Figure 3.3).

Defining processes and roles: Project planning, which includes identifying total work, estimating total effort and cost, and developing the schedule, is developed to make optimum use of all resources. Work packages and associated tasks require people from multiple disciplines to accomplish a task with a high degree of coordination. Under these circumstances, it is essential to define roles and responsibilities to bring stability and order.

Employing these formal and consistent project management *processes*: The nature of project tasks demands a multidisciplinary approach and needs people from different functions. Each person, with specific expertise and experience to the project team, contributes to the complexity

Table 3.1 People-related factors

Factor	Description
Define roles and responsibilities	At the outset, defining roles and responsibilities of project team members without ambiguity is imperative for improving performance and managing conflicts.
Create clarity in communication	Defining project goals and likely project outcomes early in the project and communicating clearly to all the team members without ambiguity.
Communicate expectations	Defining outcomes and establishing what is expected from all the team members will eventually eliminate perceived and actual incidences of not delivering expected results.
Employ consistent processes	Developing and deploying consistent and formal project management processes assist in improving operational efficiency, managing risk, and reducing ambiguity.
Build competencies	Individuals aspire to join a project team when they realize that there is an opportunity for personal and professional growth.
Establish trust	Organizational culture that promotes transparency and openness in communications would promote trust and would lead to knowledge sharing and collaboration.
Facilitate support	The project manager must have top-management support that translates into organization-wide support for the project tasks.
Manage outcomes	A clearly defined project mission statement and clear objectives help in developing a formal evaluation of project outcomes to determine project success. It promotes motivation, recognition, and team synergy.

and the project team becomes a challenging entity to manage. Employing consistent processes helps bring order to managing the project team's diverse skills representing the different disciplines. Technology plays a crucial support role in developing and deploying standard and consistent processes.

Communicating expectations and providing clarity in communication: Project managers can establish an environment of openness and transparency with effective communication of expectations, project goals, and likely project outcomes.

Facilitating support: Project managers must identify organizational support needs for the project and acquire them to effectively accomplish the expected project outcomes.

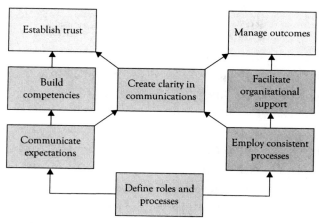

Figure 3.3 Team management and leadership process

Figure 3.3 depicts these roles by identifying the underlying relations among critical attributes of the project manager. *Defining processes and roles* is the foundation for planning and managing a project. Without such formal definition and approval of roles, projects would lack organizational and functional support. *Defining the roles and processes* would logically lead to developing formal processes. Several tools and techniques are available for developing these formal processes. Additionally, defining the roles of project team members and all the stakeholders would help both the project team members and project stakeholders understand what is expected of them. These factors help project managers define and manage project goals and outcomes. Technology's role also is important in developing, communicating, and monitoring project outcomes.

Predictability and openness are important factors in establishing trust. Furthermore, trust and communication are essential to nurture human relationships. By defining processes and roles, the project manager can establish expectations from the stakeholders and also ensure predictability and openness in communication. Together, these factors instill trust among the team members and the project manager. Establishing trust usually takes time and projects are time bound; this only adds a greater challenge. By establishing trust, the project manager can also mitigate conflicts, a deterrent to project performance.

Building competencies: Individuals aspire to join a project team when they realize that the project presents an opportunity for personal and professional growth. With challenging project work comes an opportunity to learn something new. As such, individuals should be presented with an opportunity to build competencies through mentoring, learning, and training wherever necessary. Such actions would help project managers earn the trust of team members.

Figure 3.3 shows that there is no direct relationship between establishing trust and managing outcomes. Past research studies confirm this and show that a relationship between trust and performance remains somewhat elusive in collaborative relationships. Trust has a positive, though limited, and indirect impact on performance.

People are motivated by challenges and opportunities to further their career goals. Those who are assigned to project teams are almost always interested in accomplishing personal and professional goals in addition to completing the assigned project tasks. With this in mind, project managers should inquire into the personal aspirations of the project team members and support them by defining their project roles and responsibilities. The project manager plays the role of motivating and guiding project team members for their professional growth, while completing their project-related tasks and responsibilities.

The project manager's leadership responsibility is to clearly define the project mission and to translate it into measurable project outcomes. However, many organizations do not define a formal process of evaluating project performance. Furthermore, the perception of failure and success is often based on unspoken and personal indices. The project manager must develop a set of performance indices that formalize the process and make explicitly clear what is implicit in these seemingly subjective evaluations. Without defining these measures, managing outcomes would be difficult.

Team-Performance Process

The people-related factors shown in Figure 3.3 can work both as enablers and barriers. Therefore, developing a process that represents these factors as causals, means, and effects would allow us to understand how each of these factors can act either as an enabler or a barrier to project performance (Figure 3.4).

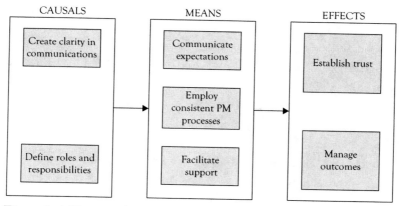

Figure 3.4 Team performance process

Establishing trust and managing outcomes are the end results or *effects*. As shown in Figure 3.4, the *means* can be controlled, manipulated, or developed to form the link between the *causals* and the *effects*. Communicating expectations, employing consistent processes, and facilitating support within the organization are the factors that can be moderated or enhanced in order to accomplish the *effects*.

The performance process shown in Figure 3.4 can be to understand the possibility of the people-related factors acting as enablers or barriers. For instance, one can argue that a robust practice of clarity in communications would help the project manager to communicate expectations at the outset of the project. On the contrary, if the project manager fails to communicate with clarity, it is unlikely that the expectations from the key stakeholders will be well conveyed. Thus, clarity in communication can act as an enabler or barrier. This argument demonstrates the dual role of all these factors either as enablers or barriers.

Project outcomes—derived from a clearly defined project mission and objectives—help to develop a formal evaluation to determine project success. Defining these outcomes and evaluating individual and team performance against them would motivate team members to perform better. Needless to say, managing these outcomes would not be possible without a clear definition of roles and processes, support from the organization, and effective communication.

Team Communication Process

Unique and new characteristics vary from project to project and are accompanied by uncertainties and unknowns, thereby influencing the difficulties associated with managing projects. Associated with uncertainty is stress that can lead to decreased motivation and participation.

One can manage uncertainty by developing a risk management plan. However, risk management alone is not sufficient to manage uncertainty. Communication plays an important role in reducing uncertainty. This is true for traditional colocated and virtual project teams. It is obvious that there are more communication challenges in virtual teams due to lack of opportunities for face-to-face and nonverbal communications.

Poor listening skills and assumptions that are made while receiving a message are the primary reasons for communication failure. Likewise, words mean different things to different people due to cultural differences. In the previous chapter, communication challenges associated with cultural differences were discussed. To circumvent the challenge associated with verbal communication, visual images are used in many public places like airports, metro transportation systems, malls, public buildings, and public places to minimize misunderstandings arising out of verbal communications and assumptions.

An array of traffic signals is the most commonly used visual communication. Imagine substituting written messages instead of red, yellow, and green light signals at road intersections and highways. It would be chaotic and a traffic nightmare!

Where verbal (oral and written) communication is used, you may encourage the receiver of the message to engage in a conversation to verify, reduce misunderstanding, and add clarity. As the receiver of the message one must consider asking questions for clarity and, as a sender, it is helpful to ask the recipient of the message to repeat how the message was understood, with specific focus on what needs to be done.

Supportive communication is critical to fostering a positive and productive interpersonal relationship. Supportive communication is the communication that seeks to preserve a positive relationship between the

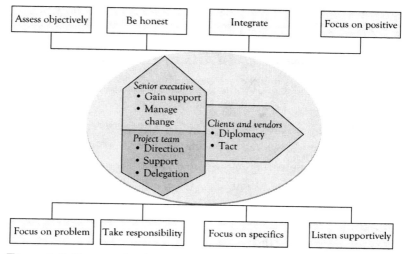

Figure 3.5 Communication process

communicators while still addressing the problem at hand.[5] Figure 3.5 shows eight attributes of supportive communication:

- *Assess objectively*: As the project manager, communicate the incidence objectively and offer a solution.
- *Be honest*: Your message, thoughts, and feelings must align completely.
- *Integrate*: Assimilate a current situation or issue at hand with the past and related communication.
- *Focus on positive*: Place emphasis on areas of agreements and strengths and communicate with respect to work collaboratively.
- *Focus on problem*: Separate the person and the issue at hand.
- *Take responsibility*: Take responsibility for your actions and words by using "I" wherever applicable.
- *Focus on specifics*: It is very important to focus on specific issues and avoid the temptation to generalize or make extreme statements.

---

[5] Whetten and Cameron (2007).

> • *Listen supportively*: Supportive listening includes the ability to listen carefully, process the message for objective understanding, and address relevant issues or concerns for an accurate understanding of the message that is conveyed.

As Figure 3.5 denotes, managers can either facilitate or constrain the free flow of information and ideas. Furthermore, open communication and tolerance for ambiguity on the part of project leadership also contribute positively to project success.

Communication with senior executives: Project-related issues with top management and senior executives tend to focus on highlighting issues, risks, and exceptions. Often the communication is formal in the form of reports. Tools used for this purpose are:

- Exception reports
- Periodic (weekly/monthly) reports
- Project charters
- E-mails
- Reviews (in person and through reports)

Communication with project team: The project manager uses status reports, and provides direction and support to the project team by means of reporting information about the project status, pending tasks, project plan updates, and progress reports. Direction and support are mostly informal and happen on a daily basis. Consequently, the communication is both formal and informal in the form of reports, routine meetings (daily/weekly), e-mail exchanges, and conversations (in person and through electronic media). The tools used for this purpose are:

- Status reports
- Meetings (daily/weekly)
- E-mails
- Reviews (in person and through reports)

Communication with external stakeholders: Periodically, the project manager and the team communicate with external stakeholders that include clients, contractors, vendors, regulatory agencies, and end users. Communication is mostly formal. Negotiation skills, emotional intelligence, conflict management, and tact are important. Tools used for this purpose are:

- Communication plan
- Contracts
- Statement of work
- Purchase orders
- Deliverable (product/service) prototypes
- Compliance reports

In a broader context, many organizations and institutions use acronyms. The use of acronyms and short-cut methods of communication is common and specific to every culture, region, country, and even the industry. Notable examples are evident in military, medical profession, air traffic control systems, and information technology (IT) software industries. This style of communication is facilitated by familiarity and results in speedy communication. Perhaps, familiarity is one of the reasons why research has shown that many organizations prefer to have contracts written in the native language.

Team Technology Process

Technology—one that facilitates knowledge sharing and knowledge transfer—plays a key role in promoting project management maturity and in improving project team performance. Historical data from the past project-planning documents, lessons learned from projects, how and why decisions are made, and communications are some of the sources of information that help to create new knowledge and to develop new systems and processes, thereby avoiding past mistakes.

In the context of managing the task-related issues of projects and project teams, technology is considered as a combination of IT and KM.

IT is effective in converting data into information, but it is not a good choice for creating knowledge. The reason is simple: Knowledge creation requires human judgment. It is imperative to define these terms:

- *Knowledge* can be derived from thinking and it is a combination of information, experience, and insight. Deriving knowledge from information requires human judgment, and is based on context and experience.
- *Knowledge management (KM)* is defined as an important strategic initiative to utilize information technology and tools, business processes, best practices, and culture to develop and share knowledge within an organization by those who possess knowledge with those who do not.

However, uncertainty increases as data are used to derive information and information is used to generate knowledge. Data are unambiguous whereas information is subject to interpretation, and knowledge is personal but very important in making decisions. Managing knowledge effectively will have a direct impact on the ability of firms to bridge the gap between IT and end users, thereby impacting organizational performance. Therefore, IT in conjunction with KM is desirable for good results.

Technology is used to denote both the IT and KM for two reasons. First, KM is considered a bridge between IT and business, and second, combining both KM and IT will facilitate knowledge sharing and provide opportunities to enhance performance in a project environment. The role of technology (IT and KM) depends on how technology systems are designed in organizations and deployed for projects. It is important that organizations develop technology systems to meet specific business and project needs. They should not be designed in isolation with the assumption that people will use it for productive purposes.

Organizations should make use of technology to store and share information and capture knowledge of past and present projects. This would help in developing better and more accurate project plans, detailed specifications, and reduce the extent and impact of uncertainties. Additionally, technology can help simplify, streamline, and standardize project management processes. It facilitates integration of complex projects and, specifically, technology plays a crucial role in managing global projects.

Technology helps design project management tools for planning and web-based support systems, which are essential for managing soft issues such as communication, conflict resolution, and knowledge sharing. The use of sophisticated project management tools, driven by factors such as project complexities and diverse cultures requiring new management skills, is having a profound impact on project leadership. Furthermore, methods of communication, decision making, soliciting commitment, and risk sharing facilitate a shift of management style to a team-centered and self-directed form of project control. Technology is essential to support this shift to participative management and the leadership of projects. Integrating project management and technology tools at every phase of the project management life cycle is desirable for both traditional and virtual project teams (Figure 3.6).

Project managers can employ technology tools to capture data and information and facilitate knowledge development and transfer. Historical project performance data can feed back into data repositories and database systems, and the result is a fluid knowledge flow between project management processes and technology tools. Project managers can achieve a level of continuous improvement in project performance by applying technology tools throughout the project management life cycle:

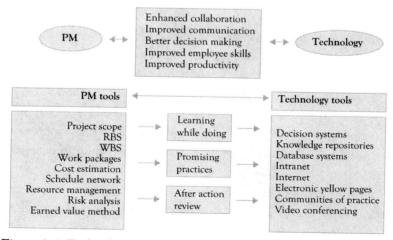

Figure 3.6 Technology and project management tools

- Selection of projects using knowledge-based decision systems
- Development of resource breakdown structure (RBS) and keeping it current with resource cost information from recently concluded projects
- Development of project plans and scope with the help of repositories
- Estimation of project costs using historical data and earned value analysis
- Development of work breakdown structure (WBS) using database systems
- Development of the project schedule using historical data and lessons learned
- Management of resources using actual resource usage data from similar projects

Technology facilitates interaction among the project team members, encourages discussions, and promotes the flow and collection of knowledge. Technology, specifically KM, promotes communication, employee skills, collaboration, decision making, and productivity. Consequently, technology (IT and KM) helps project leaders promote project performance, team development, and competency.

Furthermore, the *team management and leadership* process (Figure 3.3), discussed earlier, can be enhanced by combining with the use of technology tools (Figure 3.7).

While technology facilitates defining roles, responsibilities, and processes, it also promotes knowledge sharing, team development, efficiency, and effectiveness. However, motivating factors that can lead to knowledge sharing, team development, building competencies, and innovation are dependent on the project leadership role in establishing trust and open communication. It is here that technology plays the critical supporting role. However, one caveat to remember is that technology is not a panacea for resolving all the challenges associated with PM.

Using technology requires technical skills, and project team members must be trained to use the technology effectively. Although technology offers gains in efficiency and effectiveness, one must remember

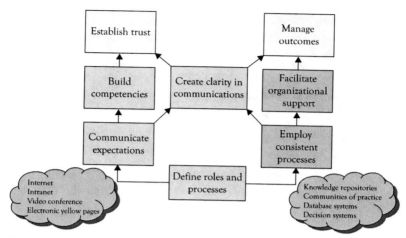

Figure 3.7 Technology process

that both the sets of technical skills and people skills are necessary and important, and that a shortfall in either can lead to a shortfall in overall performance.

Team Knowledge Management Process

Project management processes are essentially designed to be obvious and prominent. KM processes, often obscure, are integrated with project management processes to help individual and organizational learning, and provide a platform for training new people.

Developing, sharing, and retaining knowledge are part of the KM repertoire. Ultimately, leveraging this knowledge for the benefit of the organization and project teams is a critical aspect of KM. Leveraging knowledge is often manifested in learning at individual and organizational levels. Improving existing processes and implementing new processes often serve as visible evidence of organizational learning.

Akin to project management processes that are aimed to produce services, products, and results are the KM processes that are expected to create, share, and deploy knowledge within the organization and with external stakeholders. One of the important goals of a KM process is to convert tacit knowledge into organizational explicit knowledge and make it available in the right format and context to facilitate learning at individual and organizational levels. KM deals with two activities:

- Preserving and using existing knowledge, and
- Creating new knowledge for effective use

Existing knowledge includes both tacit and explicit knowledge. Creating new knowledge involves a great deal of formal and informal interaction of people with the processes and among people within the organization, which underlines the importance of developing formal and informal KM processes.

Documenting personal knowledge in some form is one of the means to share knowledge. It becomes explicit knowledge, an intellectual asset that can be shared as information within the organization. Technology plays an important supporting role in sharing knowledge, specifically in global virtual project teams.

Information exchange, one of the goals of KM, promotes collective knowledge. Organizations make people aware of the impact that their engagement in information exchanges can have on the performance of others. Another intervention is to foster cooperation by enhancing a sense of group identity and personal responsibility among team members.

Improved communication, enhanced collaboration, improved employee skills, better decision making, and improved productivity are identified as the most useful outcomes of KM[6] and all of these outcomes are of critical importance for project teams. These benefits can be identified to develop knowledge-sharing and learning processes for projects (Figure 3.8).

Figure 3.8 proposes information exchange among people within and across business processes, within and across disciplines and functions of project management to facilitate knowledge sharing and learning from each other. Furthermore, this process will facilitate the measurement of knowledge sharing among the project team members, within and across project management processes; within and across project functions; and with employee skills at task, process, project, and organization levels.

---

[6] Anantatmula (2005).

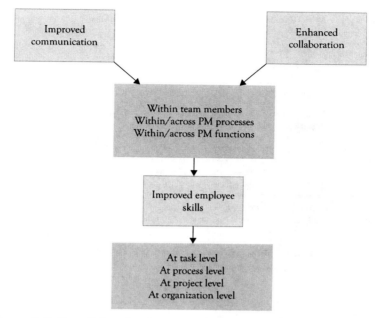

Figure 3.8 Knowledge-sharing process

Consequently, this process can facilitate individual and organizational learning.

KM functions such as storing, sharing, transferring, and converting tacit knowledge into explicit knowledge and facilitating organizational learning are some of the important responsibilities of the project management office (PMO).

Team Learning Process

Potential savings in cost and time could be significant if organizations do not resort to reinventing the wheel every time a new project is initiated. It is common knowledge that the project team can reduce project cost and duration by learning from past mistakes and making use of successful practices.

Research has shown that these lessons are not captured for various reasons (Table 3.2). Organizations must eliminate these reasons and consider incentive schemes and rewards for the project team to encourage continuous capturing of lessons learned throughout the project.

Table 3.2 Learning inhibitors

Reason	Explanation
Lack of time	Project resources are not given the time to complete lessons learned.
Lack of resources	Once the resource finishes the project task, the resource is assigned to other tasks or projects.
Lack of clear guidelines	Company processes and procedures are not well defined or enforced.
Lack of incentive	Although much effort goes into meetings, documentation, and reporting of lessons learned, the project resources are not recognized for their efforts.
Lack of management support	Functional managers and management do not see the benefit of capturing lessons learned and do not support efforts allowing their employees to participate in lessons-learned meetings and forums.

Source: Trevino and Anantatmula (2008).

The first two reasons in Table 3.2 are rooted in the management action, and the rest are the consequences of the lack of support on the part of senior management toward lessons learned. Assigning resources to another project immediately after completing a project reflects an efficient use of resources in the short term but is not an effective use of resources overall.

It is a usual practice for an organization to capture lessons learned after completing the project. However, it is desirable to capture lessons throughout the project life cycle and not just at the completion of the project (Figure 3.9), as timely capture of the information would improve project performance.

To capture lessons learned throughout the project execution, the project manager plays an important role in creating and nurturing a learning environment for capturing, analyzing, storing, disseminating, and reusing lessons learned from projects. Lessons learned should include both success and failure stories, which is not possible without establishing trust among the project team members.

With the approach depicted in Figure 3.9, the project manager and project team would seek support from peers in the organization *before the project is started* in order to learn and ascertain likely challenges of the

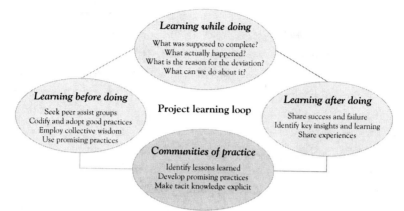

Figure 3.9 Project learning process

project such as complexity, uncertainty, and unknowns associated with similar projects. Furthermore, the team would refer to the lessons-learned databases and select relevant and promising project management practices.

While planning and executing the project, the project manager and the team would, on a daily basis, address the following questions at the end of each day:

- What was supposed to happen?
- What actually happened?
- What is the reason for the deviation?
- What can be done about it?

A rigorous and sincere effort to address these questions would help the team review plans and make amends as necessary. This approach helps the project team to recognize early warning signals and take timely corrective actions, thereby preventing cost and time overruns. This provides a basis for developing a better rationale for terminating runaway projects.

Learning while doing should not be time consuming as these questions are addressed on a daily basis. Meetings to address these questions should be short with a clear agenda. Learning after completing the project remains an important step in this process as the project manager and the team will have the benefit of a complete and comprehensive understanding of what went wrong and what went right. The experience and lessons learned will help knowledge sharing and enhance knowledge repositories. This approach would also help in carving out expertise and interest areas of project management practices and in developing communities of practices for continuous sharing of knowledge.

From a project team's perspective, a robust and effective learning process (Figure 3.10) would motivate team members to collaborate with others as it would help individuals in the team in their personal and professional growth. In this manner, team members learn from each other, achieve greater work satisfaction, improve morale, and increase productivity.

As shown in Figure 3.10, captured lessons must be analyzed to extract information that would be relevant for future projects and the current project. Once relevant information is recorded, technology that is used for storage should be easy and simple to store, access, and retrieve.

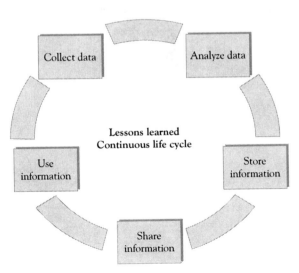

Figure 3.10 Projects lessons learned cycle

Questions:

1. Explain the difference between team processes and taskwork.
2. What characteristics does a leader need to effectively guide his team through the development process?
3. What technologies would be more appropriate for traditional project teams?
4. What technologies would be more appropriate for virtual project teams?
5. Explain effective ways to integrate project management and knowledge management disciplines.
6. What are the benefits of integrating knowledge management with project management?
7. How can a project leader implement the lessons learned in continuous life cycle?

Managing Project Teams

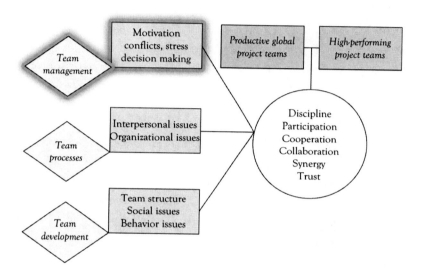

Objectives:

- Identify negative group behaviors and their impact on team performance.
- Differentiate among the various phases of social and behavioral development.
- Understand the intricate relationship between management and leadership.
- Explore motivational approaches for improving collaboration and team performance.
- Recognize the process required to prepare for negotiations.

Preview

Chapter 4 focuses on team management. It begins by illustrating the hierarchies of leadership and the necessary distances maintained between supervisors and subordinates in various cultures. The importance of delegation is discussed. Team members assume different roles and responsibilities, and not all of them are positive to team effectiveness or cohesion. This chapter details how to identify negative group behaviors, like social loafing, and how to overcome these obstacles to team performance. The chapter then goes on to cover the six-step decision-making process and how it can be used in differing situations. Groups are often required to make decisions and due to their nature, teams are subject to a variety of decision-making pitfalls. Another obstacle to team performance is conflict. Chapter 4 shows how to identify conflict, negate harmful conflict, and harness positive conflict to further the team's abilities. Closely related to conflict is the issue of team motivation. Emphasis is also placed on the different phases of behavioral and social development through the use of visual representations. The chapter concludes by showing the relationship between management and leadership. Leadership traits are required for managers to work effectively and be able to cultivate useful team relationships and to establish trust among the team members.

Captaincy is about empowerment, about making the players responsible for their actions and, in turn, accountable. It is about treating every one equally but differently by recognizing that there are varied characters who need to express their flair and inside the ultimate team vision.

—Steve Waugh

Project management, as a discipline, is still evolving. The initial emphasis on the technical skills of the project manager led to a focus on the tasks, tools, and techniques of project management. However, many research studies in the recent past underline the importance and contribution of people skills in project success, giving rise to the necessity and prominence of the project manager's management and leadership skills in managing project teams. With the emphasis shifting more toward people and behavioral skills, the project manager's personality traits, attitudes, and leadership are increasingly recognized for their role in project success and project team performance.

In this chapter, emphasis is placed on people-related issues in managing project teams. However, it does not mean that one can disregard the importance of technical skills and task-related issues and goals such as managing scope, cost, quality, and time. These are the foundational and fundamental reasons for formation of project teams.

Managing Teams—Hierarchical Structure

Although the global economy and free-market philosophy are compelling organizations to adopt lean and flat structures for efficiency and effectiveness, the power structure and perception of power equations among hierarchical levels are not experiencing corresponding changes. Contextual culture and social norms have the tendency to permeate organizations and define power equations in the organization's hierarchical structure.

Power Distance

Hofstede used the term *power distance* to explain the extent to which less powerful members of the organization accept and expect unequal distribution of power. From this perspective, organization culture can fall between *egalitarian* and *hierarchy*. In *egalitarian culture*, individuals are not set apart from the team, whereas in *hierarchy culture*, the leader is expected to be set apart from the rest of the team. In such cultures, the leader needs to set higher standards and maintain a power distance to be accepted as a leader.[1] These perceptions are influenced by the history of the nation and differences are significant (Table 4.1).

As Table 4.1 illustrates, one's approach in managing the team and communications should depend on the power distance culture. Specifically, one needs to exercise caution when dealing with people from a *hierarchy culture*. This cautious approach is generally useful to establish relations initially. Ultimately, your familiarity and adaptability with these

---

[1] Meyer (2014).

Table 4.1 Egalitarian versus hierarchy

General traits of egalitarian culture	General traits of hierarchical cultures
It is acceptable to disagree with the leader openly even in front of others	An effort is made to defer to the opinion of the leader, especially in public
People are more likely to move to action without getting approval from the leader	People are more likely to get the approval before moving to action
In meetings with clients or suppliers, less focus is on matching hierarchical levels	Hierarchy levels are strictly followed; if a manager does not attend, the senior manager would likewise not attend
It is acceptable to e-mail or call people several levels below or above one's rank	Communication follows the hierarchical chain
No protocol is required in seating or speaking with clients or partners	Seating and speaking with clients or partners follow a rigid positional protocol

Source: Adapted from Meyer (2014, 131).

two extreme cultural structures will pay rich dividends in improving team effectiveness.

In leading a project team in the Netherlands, a country with an egalitarian culture, the leader needs to be one with the team members to demonstrate equality in status and delegation of power. The opposite is true in countries like China and Japan, where it is appropriate to maintain a status and distance, and be formal in relations.

Delegation of authority, responsibility, and accountability are indicators of the power distance culture in an organization. Also, how decisions are made and who will make decisions would give one a fair indication of the power distance situation. It is not unusual to find that project teams play a role in participative or group decision making. However, in general, three scenarios of decision making emerge: the senior manager or leader makes the decision; the project team members participate in discussions, come to a conclusion, and then leave it to the manager to make a final decision; and third is a consensus decision where the project team comes to an agreement.

Delegation and decision-making style, to some extent, lets you know the power distance situation and to what extent teams are self-managed. With the increased diversity in workplaces and an opportunity to work with people from different cultures and countries in workplace, one needs to be aware of the team members' expectations of one's role and leadership style as the project manager. People from different cultures use different logical approaches, such as inductive and deductive reasons for making decisions. Flexibility and adaptability of leadership and management styles are important to one's success in leading diverse project teams and global projects.

Team Roles and Responsibilities

People are expected to play different roles in teams. A role is something a person is expected to live up to in actions and words. A role is often integrated with responsibility and accountability. Generally, these roles are classified into task, socioemotional, and destructive roles.[2]

- *Task roles*: People who play task roles are solely concerned with work and getting the job done. These team members may not be interested in understanding the big picture. As a project manager, use them for monitoring project progress and reporting status.
- *Socioemotional roles*: These roles are important for projects as these team members promote interpersonal relations such as values, feelings, and opinions about the task at hand and how to manage them. Team members who play these roles are crucial for interdependent tasks and coordination and collaborative efforts of projects.
- *Destructive roles*: As a project manager, one should also be aware of the role of a member who can sabotage the team's efforts either consciously or unconsciously. Such members should be monitored closely to curb negative emotions. These individuals require guidance and mentoring.

Delegation of responsibility is important, specifically for complex and mega projects. Project leaders should be cognizant of the aforementioned three roles and exercise caution in delegating responsibility with authority

---

[2] Eunson (2014).

and responsibility. Delegation of authority must accompany delegation of responsibility without which micromanagement could become a reality.

In the context of project teams, delegation of authority is sharing the organization's position power with other members of the team so that team members take the lead in fulfilling their roles and responsibilities without waiting for the approval of the project manager. Requiring multiple signatures for any approval suggests the absence of delegation of authority.

In matured organizations, managers know how to delegate with authority. Delegation with authority is the best way to manage teams, if the right people are in place or people have been trained to manage responsibilities independently, effectively, and efficiently. Resorting to micromanagement will not lead to good results. It is important to understand the difference and make a distinction between micromanagement and mentoring; mentoring is associated with support and guidance whereas micromanagement is associated with close supervision arising out of lack of trust and absence of belief in a subordinate's ability to carry out assigned responsibilities.

Social Loafing

Social loafing is the tendency of a team member to make less effort due to the perception that underperformance will not be noticed—thereby getting a free ride. Social loafing and withdrawal may also occur when one perceives that his or her individual effort is greater or his or her contribution is disproportionate to the rest of the team (Table 4.2).

Teams can overcome social loafing when group members become more accountable for their actions, when the activities of the group become more interesting, and when group pride is present—that is, when a group is competing with another group and group members wish to perform well and win the contest.[3] Again, delegation with authority helps to reduce social loafing, which is possible in project teams.

Defining unique roles and responsibilities would help in minimizing social loafing and it can be more easily accomplished in project teams.

---

[3] Seta, Paulus, and Baron (2000).

Table 4.2 Social loafing

Factors that increase social loafing	Factors that reduce social loafing
Lack of identity	Individual identity
No individual evaluation	Individual or group evaluation
Absence of individual/group evaluation standards	Individual or group standards of evaluation
Task is easy, boring, or same as others	Task is difficult, interesting, or different from others
Individual contributions are not necessary	Individual contributions are essential
No individual or group incentives	Individual or group incentives
Large group	Small group
Unfamiliar group	Familiar group

Source: Adapted from Seta, Paulus, and Baron (2000, 218).

Furthermore, most of the factors that reduce social loafing, as outlined in Table 4.2, can be included in the design of project teams. Specifically, project tasks are usually difficult, challenging, and different from others due to the triple constraints of scope, cost, and duration. Also, individual contributions are essential and recognized in projects.

Decision Making in Teams

Primary education and how people are trained to think influence their thought process and decision making. Project leaders often find themselves working with people from around the world, and with varying educations and philosophies. So, it is not easy to convince everyone in the team to adapt one style of reasoning.

Group decisions are made either by reaching consensus or by a top-down approach. Arriving at a consensus may take a long time but implementation is greatly facilitated. In a top-down approach, decisions are often made quickly but may lead to more discussions during implementation and the decision could be subjected to revisions.

Cultural Issues of Decision Making

Using logic to make decisions is based on either deductive or inductive reasoning principles. People from countries with a long history, such as

Italy, Spain, France, Germany, and Russia, derive conclusions from general principles or concepts, also known as *deductive reasoning* or *principles-first reasoning*. Thus, the focus is on understanding the reason behind the doing (why). On the other hand, people from countries like the United States, United Kingdom, Canada, and Australia, employ *Inductive Reasoning or applications-first reasoning*. These individuals derive conclusions based on a pattern of factual observations from the world using their sensory organs such as hearing, visualizing, and imagining. In doing so, their focus is on learning from the experience and experimentation (how).

Oriental societies like Japan, China, and India and the countries influenced by their cultures tend to live in harmony with nature and prefer harmonious relations and consensus in making decisions. People from these cultures derive conclusions using both deductive and inductive reasoning from a holistic or system's perspective while assigning greater importance to harmony in teams.

Depending on the situation, everyone is capable of using both the reasoning styles and the holistic view in decision making. However, the general tendency is to follow one of these reasoning styles based on training from one's primary education. Furthermore, one's discipline (engineering, science, philosophy, psychology, etc.) also influences his or her reasoning style.

As the project manager, all the three approaches should be used in making decisions. To implement these decisions or encourage people to participate in the decision-making process, the project manager needs to develop skills in persuading team members by using one or a combination of all the three approaches. One's success in persuading others largely depends on the ability to switch among different reasoning styles, which in turn depends on the context, diversity in culture and discipline, team size, composition, and structure.

To increase effectiveness of decisions in multicultural or large project teams, consider forming subgroups of like-minded people or people from similar cultures or the same culture. From a decision-making perspective, cultural diversity helps if the goal is innovation or creativity; however, if the team's goal is to accomplish the task fast and with efficiency, consider reducing the cultural diversity in the team.

In the current global economy of workplace diversity and virtual work environments, understanding the effects of cultural diversity on decision making assumes significance. The project manager needs to implement a group decision-making process that encourages participation from all the relevant parties and evaluates decisions based on set criteria that are tied to project deliverables.

Behavioral Issues of Decision Making

Standard economic theory is based on the premise that people make rational decisions. It assumes that when making decisions, one is informed and the approach is logical and sensible to maximize value. However, accessing and evaluating complete information are impossible. Behavioral economics expert Dan Ariely argues that our decisions are influenced by several irrational impulses, which are systematic and predictable. These influences come from our immediate environment, unrelated emotions, shortsightedness, and other forms of irrationality. It would make a better sense if economics concepts were based on how people actually behave.

Decision-Making Process

A project team's effectiveness and its leader's success would largely depend on the value and impact of their decisions. Leaders often are made or broken by their decisions.[4] A shift from the *classic view* of decision making—one time event based on experience, intuition, and research—to an ongoing process of decision making that overlooks larger social and organizational contexts is desirable for project teams.

Research has shown that viewing decision making as a process leads to better decisions. It is desirable to have an open process to identify and evaluate all alternatives, encourage participation to foster the exchange of ideas, and develop a valid decision that solves problem at hand. This approach is likely to encourage open, objective, creative, innovative, and quality solutions. The decision-making process involves the following steps:

---

[4] Garvin and Roberto (2001).

1. *Identify the problem*: Define the problem at hand, develop goals, and gather relevant information.
2. *Develop objective criteria*: Criteria must be aligned with project goals and they should be specific, measurable, and achievable (reasonable).
3. *Generate all possible solutions*: A team's cultural diversity can be of advantage in generating several possible solutions.
4. *Select the best option*: Employ various qualitative and quantitative decision-making techniques such as analytical hierarchy process, decision tree analysis, and expected monetary value to select the most suitable option.
5. *Implement the chosen option*: Assess the resources required for implementing the selected option as planned.
6. *Monitor results*: Outcomes of the decision must be monitored to ensure that intended results are accomplished.

Of these steps, making a distinction between the problem (core issue) and the symptom and addressing the problem sets you in the right direction. To illustrate the importance of addressing the right problem, consider the crime rate in a major city. If one considers crime as the problem, a logical conclusion would be to reinforce crime control by deploying more police force and increase vigilance. However, if the root cause or the problem is considered to be income disparity and poverty, redefining economic policies addresses the core issue.

Decision Making in Projects

Projects are often associated with uncertainties and unknowns. Uncertainty is associated with tentative nature where one cannot be definitive about the outcome of an event. Project risk is an uncertain event or a condition that, if occurs, has a positive or a negative effect on at least one project objective. Consequently, project teams make four types of decisions: decision making under certainty, decision making under uncertainty, decision making with risk, and decision making with lack of information (unknowns). Of these, it is preferable to use groups for the last three types of decisions.

A project manager should guard against some of the issues that hinder making decisions, which are lack of accurate and real information, and unrealistic assumptions, opinions, and biases. The group decision-making approach, if developed well, can minimize or eliminate some or all of these weaknesses. Group decision making has the advantage of collective wisdom, analyzing the problem from different perspectives, and healthy and detailed discussion of the issue at hand. Furthermore, group decision making makes sense in project teams as team members represent multiple disciplines and diverse experiences. In addition, global project teams represent different cultural perspectives and associated diversity in expertise and experience in making effective decisions, if interpersonal conflicts are managed well.

Perils of Group Decision Making

The quality of decisions is often influenced by organizational politics, power struggles, work ethics, and organizational culture. Absence of delegation and accountability would adversely affect decisions. Groupthink causes people to make suboptimal decisions when cohesion is very high and when individuals like each other. Members of the team would become uncomfortable to question the group consensus even if the decision is objectionable.

While making decisions, people are often engaged in rigorous debate due to critical thinking and in-depth analysis of the problem at hand. For these reasons, the decision-making process is often associated with conflicts.

Conflicts and Conflict Management

Conflict is the result of a difference of perception, opinion, or beliefs among people. Usually, conflict occurs when there are incompatible goals, thoughts, or emotions between individuals or groups, which result in opposition and disagreements.

Types of Conflict

Conflicts are often categorized as *cognitive* or *affective*.[5]

---

[5] Garvin and Roberto (2001).

Cognitive conflict refers to disagreements and different ideas that are associated with the work. In other words, it is a task-related conflict. Cognitive conflict leads to healthy and desired discussions. Such conflict is often productive and must be encouraged during the decision-making process.

Affective conflict is interpersonal and emotional conflict. It arises out of personal differences and personality clashes. It is also known as people-related conflict. This conflict reduces participation and cooperation in the decision-making process.

Cognitive and *affective* conflicts are interpersonal and occur at an individual level. Similar to *affective conflict*, past studies recognize a conflict in a team known as *relationship conflict*; it refers to interpersonal incompatibility and friction among team members and it is an outcome of team disagreements that are characterized by feelings of personality clash, anger, hostility, dislike, frustration, and distrust among team members.[6] *Relationship conflict* results in tension, annoyance, and animosity.[7] Obviously, *relationship conflict* is a people-related conflict and not a task-related conflict.

Culture and Conflict

The cultures of various countries influence how people are predisposed to confront an issue and express emotions. Japan and Indonesia prefer to avoid confrontation, whereas on the other extreme, Israel and France prefer confrontation to resolve disagreement.[8] Erin Meyer observes that France is emotionally expressive in confrontation, whereas Germany is not. Likewise, Japan is emotionally unexpressive in avoiding confrontation, whereas India is emotionally expressive. Establishing trust among the team members, specifically in global project teams, would help in these situations but it takes time; project teams are temporary and project

---

[6] Furumo (2009); Hinds and Bailey (2003).

[7] Jehn (1995).

[8] Meyer (2014).

durations may not be long enough to instill trust among the team members. It is a paradox with which every project must deal.

Diverse View of Conflict in Projects

Over the years, three different views have developed about conflict in projects and organizations.[9]

- The *traditional view* of conflict suggests that conflict is negative and must be avoided and it is a manager's responsibility to create a culture that fosters harmony.
- The *behavioral view* still considers conflict as mainly negative, but it also believes that it is natural and inevitable. Managers are encouraged to manage conflict instead of eliminating it. This view also accepts the fact that conflict can yield positive results if managed properly.
- The *interactionist view* believes that conflict should be encouraged up to a certain level because it is necessary to improve performance. Low levels of conflict can lead to less innovation, less change, and fewer improvements for the organization.

In a project management context, it is desirable to adapt the *behavioral view* or *interactionist view* to manage conflicts and promote creativity in problem solving.

Conflicts in Projects and Project Teams

Conflicts in projects are complex, arising out of project management processes, project-related issues, personality differences, and culture (Table 4.3).

However, people, rather than tasks, processes, and procedures, play a greater role in causing dysfunctional conflicts that could lead to devastating and long-lasting effects on interpersonal relations. If interpersonal

---

[9] Robbins (1979a); Robbins and Stuart-knotze (1986).

Table 4.3 Sources of conflict

People	Project facets
Personality attributes • Ethics • Civility • Trust • Commitment • Communication • Attitude • Integrity	**Project** • Resources • Cost • Duration • Schedule • Risk • Scope • Quality
Culture • Individual • Society • Organization • Nation	**Project management** • Processes/procedures • Practices • Standards • Policies

Source: Adapted from Rad and Anantatmula (2010).

conflict is not managed promptly, it could become intense, personal, emotional, subjective, and difficult to resolve. Ultimately, it could cause employee absenteeism and turnover. Obviously, such a conflict would be detrimental to team performance and project success. Emotional intelligence helps you put yourself in others' shoes and consider the perspective of others. It is key to reducing or eliminating people-related conflicts and helps in communicating effectively. Additional information on emotional intelligence will be provided later.

A conflict impacts performance, and poor performance influences conflict. As such, task- or project-related conflicts also impact performance. However, project-related conflicts would have a positive impact if the team is managed in an environment characterized by high levels of trust, openness, and psychological safety. Conflict associated with project tasks encourages creativity and innovation if managed well and rationality is maintained.

A project-related conflict can also be instigated to bring out sensitive issues to the team members for a healthy discussion and debate while not interfering and allowing conflict resolution to come naturally. If managed well, conflict facilitates team development and maturity. However, letting the team resolve the conflict is not a good idea when the team is comprised of people from different countries representing diverse cultural values.

Conflict Management Strategies

Project managers may consider several approaches to manage conflict and the selected approach would depend on the nature of the conflict:

- *Forcing*: using formal authority or other power to satisfy his or her concerns without regard to the concerns of the other party.
- *Accommodating*: allowing the other party to satisfy its concerns while neglecting his or hers.
- *Avoiding*: not paying attention to the conflict and not taking any action to resolve it.
- *Compromising*: attempting to resolve a conflict by identifying a solution that is partially satisfactory to both parties, but completely satisfactory to neither.
- *Collaborating*: cooperating with the other party to understand its concerns and expressing his or her concerns in an effort to find a mutually and completely satisfactorily solution.

Of these, the last two strategies are significant in managing project and project team conflicts. The project manager can employ different approaches for *compromising* and *collaborating* to make effective decisions. Some of the proven practices are engaging the team in a vigorous debate while establishing norms for the debate, challenging the accepted resolutions, dividing the project team into two groups that would present counter arguments, and assigning a controversial and out-of-box thinking team member for the role of devil's advocate. *Compromising* and *collaborating* strategies offer mutually agreeable approaches to resolving a conflict, and negotiation can be used as a process.

Negotiations

Everyone within the project management discipline, who is either involved with projects or project teams, negotiates about important project issues on a daily basis: yet almost no one recognizes that he or she is using negotiation methods or skills.

Negotiation is defined as the principal way to redefine an old relationship that is not working effectively or to establish a new relationship. Obviously, people represent both the parties in negotiations. Negotiation is the most commonly used process to resolve a dispute or a difference between two individuals or parties. However, negotiation must be preceded by influence.

Influence refers to the ability to change or affect the actions or thoughts of other people. The definition refers to other terms such as social influence, peer pressure, charisma, connections, and other descriptions that are commonly used to describe the ability to get things done.

Project managers tend to be assiduous negotiators as their performance and consequent project success depend on their ability to influence others to cooperate and perform. Whether bargaining for resources with organizational leaders, drawing up contracts, managing stakeholders, or dealing with project sponsors, project managers spend an inordinate amount of time seeking concessions from others in order to complete projects successfully.

Project managers must be skilled at negotiations as negotiations are pervasive throughout the field of project management. Negotiations are also used to manage or resolve conflicts (or made more severe) within the conflict-prone environment that is integral to project management. To initiate negotiations, certain conditions must exist (Table 4.4).

Preferably, all the conditions listed in the Table 4.4 must exist for healthy negotiations. The absence of any of these conditions can potentially derail the negotiation process and may adversely affect the outcome by intensifying the differences. Negotiations often influence the extent of success or failure in the results of any project (Table 4.5).

The steps outlined in Table 4.4 are the recommended sequence of stages in negotiations to accomplish desired outcomes. Negotiation can lead to various outcomes; it is a process of managing and resolving disputes, developing agreements that are acceptable to both the parties, bargaining for individual or collective advantage, and crafting outcomes to satisfy various interests of both the parties.

In a typical functional organization, project managers have very little power or actual authority. Even in the projectized and matrix

Table 4.4 Negotiation

Getting to yes
Getting to yes introduces a method of negotiating that centers on the identification of problems and development of solutions that all parties find acceptable. It is comprised of four elements that build upon each other to direct efforts at finding solutions instead of laying blame.
1. **Separate the people from the problem**—once the problem has been removed from the equation, and focus is shifted to the problem, working with the people and understanding them and the problem would be easier.
2. **Focus on interests and not positions**—identify the interest of all parties with a tough stand on dealing with the problem but be cooperative and gentle with people.
3. **Invent options for mutual gain**—use decision-making tools and techniques to create collectively acceptable solutions.
4. **Insist on the use of objective criteria**—Develop criteria that take into account all the interests and goals and then work together to select the best option.

Source: Fisher, Ury, and Patton (2011).

Table 4.5 Conditions for negotiations

Identifiable parties, willing to negotiate	No psychological barriers to settlement
Both the parties must have a stake	Issues must be negotiable
Inclination to negotiate	People must have authority to decide
Agreement on some issues and interests	A willingness to compromise
Motivation to settle	Agreement must be reasonable
Unpredictability of outcome	Favorable external factors for settlement
A sense of urgency and deadline	Resources to negotiate
Means of influence or leverage	

Source: Adapted from Moore (n.d.).

organizational structures, negotiations, in obtaining organizational priority, resources, and funds, are of similar importance. These concerns make it all the more important for a project manager's ability to influence others and to negotiate successfully. Influencing and negotiating skills are the project manager's strengths to obtain project resources, cooperation and support of all the key stakeholders. Influencing is the less obvious, more indirect path of the two skills, yet both are indispensable strategies for effectiveness in managing projects.

One should realize that negotiation could often be precluded by judicious application of influence. If others can be persuaded to serve the interests of the project manager, then the need for negotiation is reduced. At times, a powerful influencing strategy may be a type of informal or even unspoken "wheeling and dealing" process between the project manager and various stakeholders. It is incumbent on project managers to be creative in applying their influence and negotiation skills in order to get the best for the project. However, a project manager should be mindful that, under certain circumstances, negotiations may have to be avoided altogether (Table 4.6).

One must mitigate the issue or issues listed in Table 4.6 or avoid the negotiation. Most project managers do not even recognize when a negotiation has the potential of sabotaging or salvaging the project. Also, it is unrealistic to believe that all the negotiations are handled well in any project. The project manager must continuously communicate with all the stakeholders in the project environment because:

- The scope of the project changes and evolves,
- People are moved into and out of the project team, and
- Prior estimates and promises are proven to be wrong or unattainable.

The project manager cannot afford to lose these negotiations. However, few of us truly understand what a negotiation is, and fewer still have ever studied the negotiation process. However, one must understand that

Table 4.6 Reasons for avoiding negotiations

Confers legitimacy to an adversary	Lack of confidence in the negotiation process
Fearful of being perceived as weak	Lack of jurisdictional authority
Discussions are still premature	Authoritative powers are reluctant to meet
Will provide false hope	Is too time consuming
Might increase undesirable visibility of dispute	Need additional time to prepare
Could intensify dispute	Scope to escalate conflict and gain

Source: Adapted from Moore (n.d.).

negotiations involve a process that is really quite simple to understand. Traits and skills required for negotiations are:

- Openness and transparency in communication to establish trust
- Open mind to accept new ideas and solutions
- Ability to understand other points of view
- Attention to detail
- Creativity

Interest-based bargaining[10] is a desirable approach to negotiations. It involves a collaborative effort to meet needs and satisfy mutual interests of both the parties. Rather than moving from positions to counter positions for a compromise, negotiators pursuing an interest-based bargaining approach attempt to identify their interests or needs and those of other parties prior to developing specific solutions. Then the negotiators jointly search for a variety of settlement options that might satisfy the interests of the parties involved in the negotiations. This approach to negotiation is also referred to as integrated bargaining due to its emphasis on cooperation, a focus on mutual needs, and the effort to develop a wiser decision.

Motivation

Motivating is the process of getting others to willingly do the tasks that are required to be completed. It is a person's desire and commitment, and how he or she manifests in a job-related effort. Obviously, motivated people do things not because they have to do them but because they want to do so. Needless to say, a person's commitment is bound to be greater if doing the work out of a desire to do so, thereby improving the efficiency and effectiveness of the work performed. However, motivating people is not easy. A recent study by the Kellogg School of Management suggested that developing and sustaining motivation is considered the most frustrating and challenging aspect of teamwork.[11]

---

[10] Moore (n.d.).
[11] Thompson (2014).

It is argued that motivation has to come from within. To achieve this, the project manager must align the team member's personal aspirations with team roles and responsibilities. However, as the project manager, one can also influence and create work conditions that would generate the necessary drive to do the work enthusiastically. Generally, a person's desire to do well is based on two factors: the need for success and a fear of failure (Figure 4.1).

A low fear of failure and a high need for success encourages people to experiment with new approaches, thereby enhancing team learning. The project manager can assign team members to challenging and new technology-related tasks where unknowns and uncertainties are high.

On the other hand, people with a high fear of failure and a high need for success tend to be detail oriented, calculated, pragmatic, and motivated to excel at what they do. It is helpful to assign such people for project planning, monitoring and control, and risk planning.

In general, it is important to motivate people who have a low need for success, a high fear of failure, or both.

Motivating the project team involves getting the team members to do the tasks that need to be done. This is best accomplished when team members understand the value of the work in the overall success of the project and are committed to doing these tasks to ensure project success. If people want to do the required tasks and are committed to the project

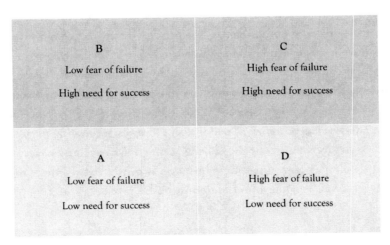

Figure 4.1 Drivers of motivation

success, the job is likely to be accomplished much better than relying on forced compliance to do the work.

The motivation of teams can also be accomplished by external means such as devising a suitable incentive scheme for individuals and groups. If performance and the source of contribution cannot always be easily assigned to an individual in a project team, distribution of an incentive or group reward is the norm. In a team, the interdependency of task assignments, team structure, and the close working relations among team members may make each member's effort more visible to peers. In such a case, if an incentive scheme based on team performance is in place, individuals within the team have an incentive to monitor and be monitored by other members in the team, which can have a powerful supervisory impact on the overall team productivity.[12]

Managing Teams During Behavioral Phases

To earn trust from the project team members, it is necessary to develop an ability to understand the viewpoints of others by placing yourself in their shoes, sharing their feelings, and demonstrating an understanding of their feelings. This is known as empathy. It is also important to understand the difference between sympathy and empathy.

Sympathy and Empathy
Sympathy is the ability to express or share other's feelings arising out of grief or a difficult situation. Sympathy is accompanied by the offer of help or advice about a positive solution to the current plight.
Empathy is one's ability to assume someone else's position, understand, and relate as best as possible so as to understand how that person feels in the situation. Empathy has to be accompanied by the trait of being able to express this feeling and understanding.
Empathy is accomplished by being honest and listening actively without judgment. Empathy helps to build trust and understanding that are healthy and positive for both people.

As a manager, developing empathy is one of the first initiatives to establish an open and honest communication. It also helps toward building trust among the team members.

---

[12] Barua, Lee, and Whinston (1995).

In Chapter 2, social and behavior issues in developing teams were discussed. Five stages of behavior phases—self-identity, social identity, group emotion, group mood, and emotional intelligence—were presented and associated with the team development process. Aligning these five behavioral phases with the team development phases of forming, storming, norming, and performing stages would present a strategic leadership and management approach to enhancing project team effectiveness from behavioral perspective (Figure 4.2 and Table 4.7).

Forming Stage

Team members are at the *self-identity* stage and do not identify with the team or its work culture. The typical interpersonal behaviors that signal this stage are silence, self-consciousness, dependence, and superficiality. Helping team members become acquainted with one another and with their collective goals and responsibilities should be the primary objectives at this stage of development. During this stage, as a leader of the team, one should be observant about negative emotions and curtail them. It is beneficial to adopt a directive leadership style.

Storming Stage

During this stage, team members are in the process of developing a social identity where individuals in the team derive their self-perceptions from affiliation with the team. The key issues to be addressed at this stage

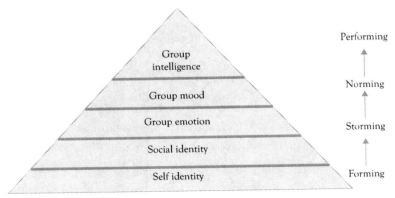

Figure 4.2 Hierarchy of social and behavioral development

Table 4.7 Team behavior characteristics and management

Social/behavioral stage	Individual/team characteristics	Effective management style	Project manager's role
Self-identity Forming stage	Focus on self Low team cohesion	High directive management	• Meet one-on-one to assess skill levels • Use assertive social behaviors to establish leadership • Establish clear social and behavioral rules and expectations • Encourage politeness • Demonstrate intolerance for minority bias and nonacceptance of ideas
Social identity Storming stage	Focus on team member Low team cohesion	High directive and low supportive management	• Demonstrate positive emotions to convey leadership • Address negative behaviors that result in power or status struggles • Maintain awareness of an individual's tendency to withdraw from team • Match the individual's social and behavioral attributes to meaningful tasks
Group emotion Norming stage	Focus team with a shift to team process Medium team cohesion	Medium directive and supportive management	• Encourage formation of friendships • Create opportunities for increased interaction with virtual teams • Maintain personal positive emotion to maintain leadership status • Encourage positive emotions and discourage negative emotions
Group mood Norming stage Performing stage	Focus on team process Medium team cohesion	Low directive and high supportive management	• Monitor the team for signs of emerging negative behaviors and high/ low emotional states • Intervene when negative behaviors are exhibited • Maintain awareness of social loafing tendencies
Emotional intelligence Performing stage	Focus on the individual's thoughts/feelings High team cohesion Team functions as one entity	Team is self-managed	• Monitor team behaviors and promote creativity • Maintain team awareness of project mission • Minimize intervention to allow for natural progression of team process

include managing conflicts, legitimizing productive expressions of individuality, turning counterdependence into interdependence, and fostering consensus-building processes. This can be facilitated by maintaining flexibility within the team, focusing on common objectives and a common vision, reinforcing commitment and values, and encouraging team members to teach and learn from one another.

Norming Stage

During this stage, personal emotions can be elevated to a group level to transform into *group emotion*. Furthermore, these group emotions are naturally extended into the next level of *group mood* as project teams make progress with the team development. Key issues that need to be addressed at this stage include roles and responsibilities, participation and empowerment, interdependent support, feedback systems, and the decision-making processes. The typical interpersonal behaviors that signal this stage are cooperativeness, conformity to standards and expectations, heightened interpersonal attraction, and ignoring disagreements.

The perils of groupthink need to be avoided or prevented at this stage. Groupthink occurs when members feel invulnerable, discredit disconfirming information, rationalize away threats, use morality to rationalize their "right" decisions, keep silent about misgivings, impose sanctions on dissenting members, keep disturbing ideas from consideration, and possess illusions of unanimity and consensus. To avoid or prevent groupthink, teams should have critical evaluators, open discussions, subgroups, outside experts, a devil's advocate, and second-chance meetings, where "second thoughts" can be raised. Other actions in the storming stage of development can help teams overcome groupthink tendencies. During this stage, the team leader should create opportunities for team members to understand each other and adopt a high directive and low supportive leadership style.

Performing Stage

The project team continues to mature and perform at higher levels as group mood is elevated even further to the level of emotional intelligence. The typical interpersonal behaviors that signal this stage are high mutual trust, unconditional commitment to the team, mutual training and development, and entrepreneurship. Once individuals and groups experience truly high levels of performance, team members are unlikely to be satisfied with mediocre or average levels of performance. This is the change that leaders can help bring about in a successful team.

Personality Dimensions of a Project Manager

The project manager has many facets and roles in managing projects. The project manager and the project team play significant roles in project performance. Several research studies investigated project success and the soft skills of the project manager. Required traits and attitudes of the project manager to manage project teams effectively are identified[13] in Table 4.8.

Table 4.8 Personality traits and attitudes

Trait and attitude	Description
Communication apprehension	An individual's level of fear or anxiety associated with either real or anticipated communication with others.
Innovativeness	The innovativeness (innovation orientation) refers to the degree to which leaders promote innovation orientation of subordinates. A team's innovativeness is a capacity that incorporates receptivity to new ideas, products, or processes, as well as an increased likelihood of their implementation or adoption.
Self-monitoring	Self-monitoring is an internal process of assessing the environment and situations and adjusting one's behavior such as verbal and nonverbal communication, emotions, and self-presentations to present a positive and desirable public appearance.
Conflict management	Conflict is the result of a difference of perception, opinion, or beliefs among people. Usually, conflict occurs when there are incompatible goals, thoughts, or emotions between individuals that result in opposition and disagreements. Conflict management refers to managing real or perceived differences effectively.
Change initiation	Change is an intervention to modify an existing practice or functioning of an organization. Often change is associated with uncertainty and complexity, and it is necessary for progress. Change initiation refers to influencing and encouraging others to adopt new practices.
MBTI personality	The Myers–Briggs Type Indicator (MBTI) is a self-assessment tool to determine cognitive styles, and certain styles are better suited to manage projects well.

[13] Creasy and Anantatmula (2013).

Communication Apprehension

Communication is considered a critical success factor for managing projects successfully. Strong project managers may spend up to 80 percent of their time communicating with team members and project stakeholders.[14] Communication apprehension is appropriate due to the type and depth of communication that a project manager has to deal with routinely. Project managers experiencing a high degree of context communication apprehension during group discussions and formal meetings are less likely to experience project success than those project managers with a low-context communication apprehension.

Innovativeness

Project teams often face the challenge of completing the project with competing constraints, which essentially require innovation to achieve project success. Furthermore, project plans undergo changes and, many times, you need to be creative in managing these changes while completing the project on time and within budget.

The project manager has to lead the team by initiating and considering pragmatic innovative ideas and, therefore, the degree of innovativeness possessed by a manager is considered an important trait. Project managers with a significant penchant toward innovativeness will experience more project success than those project managers with little to no innovative inclinations.

Self-Monitoring

Project managers perform multiple roles such as manager, leader, change agent, facilitator, innovator, negotiator, and communicator. In performing these roles, it is important for the project manager to maintain a positive image to influence the project team and stakeholders, and the concept of self-monitoring is necessary. Project managers with low self-monitoring

---

[14] Whetten and Cameron (2011).

will engage in little surface acting and therefore will experience less withdrawal, burnout, and so on, thereby producing more project success.

Conflict Management

Conflict is often an integral component of project management work. Often, conflicts are necessary for project teams to develop and mature. An understanding of conflict management styles of project managers is considered important for managing projects successfully. Project managers who practice the behavioral view of conflict, the *interactionist view* of conflict, or both, will experience more project success than those managers practicing the traditional view. In other words, project managers who encourage conflicts up to a certain level to improve performance are likely to experience project success.

Change Initiation

Instituting change to project management processes, systems, and project deliverables is an important attribute of managing projects successfully and, therefore, a project manager's propensity to manage or initiate change is included as an important attribute. Project managers who are inclined toward instituting change within their projects (as it pertains to product innovation, process reengineering, and so forth) will experience more project success than those project managers who are not.

Personality Type

Finally, an examination of the importance of project manager personality type using the MBTI assessment seems necessary. Research has shown that project managers with MBTI classifications—INTJ, ESTJ, and ENTJ—will enjoy more project success.[15] Project managers with an inclination toward instituting change in general are more equipped in project management planning and, therefore, will experience greater levels of project success.

---

[15] Gehring (2007).

Management and Leadership

Managers are people who do things right, while leaders are people who do the right thing.

—Warren Bennis

In Chapter 2, the difference between management and leadership roles was discussed. To reiterate, management is usually focused on classical functions such as planning, organizing, and controlling. In general, management is concerned with making decisions about processes and functions in order to improve operational efficiency and effectiveness. Leadership, on the other hand, is about motivating and guiding people to realize their potential and achieve tougher and challenging organizational goals.

Among the leadership styles, situational leaders focus on various tasks and relationship behaviors, and transformational leaders may inspire followers, meet their developmental needs, and encourage new approaches and more effort toward problem solving. One may argue that the transactional leadership style, which is based on the exchange of reward and work, is more suited to organizational processes, whereas transformational leadership is useful when one is concerned with relations. As the project manager, it is necessary to switch from a transactional to transformational leadership style depending on the situation at hand.

Different project leadership styles are appropriate at different stages of the project life cycle[16] and this would also depend on the characteristics of the project at hand. Although leadership style and competence are key success factors to a manager's business performance, past research did not suggest a correlation between leadership style and competence, and project success.

The project manager has a leadership role in creating an effective working environment for the project team. In the context of project management and project teams, leaders are required to assign appropriate

---

[16] Turner and Müller (2005).

importance to relationships and to communicate core values while likewise assigning appropriate attention to project management processes.

For a time-constrained project, task focus is important and a military-trained leadership style, which has a greater emphasis on completing tasks on time (failure is not an option), often works better. It does not mean that military-style leadership does not work in other circumstances. For instance, military officers are also trained to be very empathetic.

For a resource-constrained project, one may adopt a different leadership style that depends on the project and situation. Project size, type (uniqueness), uncertainties, and unknowns are some of the characteristics that would influence a project manager's leadership style. Also, organization structure and virtual teams may require the project manager to adopt a new approach to leadership style.

A recent survey[17] of 189,000 people in 81 diverse (in geography, industry type, and size) organizations around the world was conducted to assess leadership behaviors. Results suggested that high-quality leadership teams displayed four behaviors that explained the differences between strong and weak organizations with respect to leadership effectiveness (Table 4.9).

Identifying the right problem, not the symptoms, is key to problem solving and decision making. Many times, people are found solving the wrong problem without recognizing the root cause. For example, although it is necessary, beefing up law enforcement agencies cannot control crime rate in a society; a permanent solution lies in appropriate economic and related policies to address income disparity.

Likewise, project plans and decisions should be made with a focus on their results and consequences. A comprehensive and holistic approach such as system analysis is desirable in developing project plans. In managing difficult situations or complex problems, leaders must encourage participation to share ideas and develop resolutions. An exhaustive long-term plan must be in place for the development of skills and expertise

---

[17] Feser, Mayol, and Srinivasan (2015).

Table 4.9 Leadership effectiveness

Leadership effectiveness
Solving problems effectively The process that precedes decision making is identifying the problem and finding an appropriate solution. Once a problem is identified, information is gathered, analyzed, and considered. This is not easy, but it is a key input into decision making.
Operating with a strong results orientation Leadership is not only about developing and communicating a vision and setting objectives but also transforming the vision and objectives into tasks to achieve results. Leaders with a strong results orientation tend to emphasize the importance of efficiency and productivity.
Seeking different perspectives A leader should be unbiased and objective in approaching a problem or difficult situation. It is important to encourage employees to share their ideas that could improve performance, differentiate between important and unimportant issues, and to give the appropriate weight to stakeholder concerns.
Supporting others Leaders must be supportive in understanding and sensing how other people feel. By showing authenticity and a sincere interest in those around them, leaders build trust and inspire and help everyone to overcome challenges.

Source: Feser, Mayol, and Srinivasan (2015).

among the people to develop future leaders, sustain growth, and attain project management maturity.

Developing Trust

Openness and transparency in communication instill trust among the project team members. Establishing trust is an important leadership role of a project manager. Trust can be developed by defining individual roles and responsibilities; communicating expectations; identifying training needs for task-related skills and professional growth; and helping team members to build competencies through training, mentoring, and other learning opportunities.

Furthermore, team members must work together, support each other's work, share problems and find solutions together, make decisions collectively, and resolve conflicts among themselves and with the management. All these actions, along with social and informal meeting opportunities, facilitate a greater understanding among all the members that will help develop a bond and trust among the team members and with the leader.

Trust encourages project team members to collaborate, network, and innovate. Trust is more important for leaders to motivate others to accomplish a vision and achieve project goals. By establishing trust, leaders can manage changes and mitigate conflicts, a deterrent to project performance, and transform project stakeholders into a cohesive project team. Another important responsibility of the project leadership is to define the project mission clearly and translate it into measurable project outcomes.

> **Importance of the leader**
>
> If you build an army of 100 lions and their leader is a dog, in any fight, lions will die like a dog. But if you build an army of 100 dogs and their leader is a lion, all dogs will fight like a lion.
>
> —Napoleon Bonaparte

Issues That Can Derail the Team

Absence of trust, fear of conflict, lack of commitment, avoiding accountability, and not paying enough attention to results are considered as dysfunctions of a team.[18] Furthermore, measures of performance and motivational issues, if not handled well, can hinder team performance (Table 4.10).

Table 4.10 Pitfalls of management

Pitfalls of popular management issues
Measurement of performance   People, by virtue of their self-awareness, are aware when you try to measure their performance and make it exactly look like the way you would want it to be. People optimize for metrics of performance, thereby sacrificing quality (Austin 1996). Metrics can have an adverse effect on productive teams.
Motivation   Intrinsic motivation is an inherent desire for good performance. Often managers offer extrinsic motivation by offering financial or other rewards for good performance. Encouraging and nurturing intrinsic motivation lead to productivity in the long term. Instead, the focus should be to create intrinsic motivation.

---

[18] Lencioni (2002).

In addition to the issues discussed in the previous section about establishing trust, the project manager can instill trust and understanding through the discussion of vulnerabilities and revealing personal weaknesses among the team members.

To avoid the fear of conflict, team meetings should be informative, insightful, and interesting with established norms that encourage active participation. Team meetings and discussions should not intimidate people.

As the leader and project manager, one must ensure that every member of the team is committed to improving the team performance and no one is doing more work than others. The entire team should be aware of this level of commitment. The team members must be collectively committed toward the team's goal by focusing on the results required to reach the overall objective of the project. If results are not up to par, a discussion must be held to learn from it. Team members should hold one another accountable for their required contributions toward a project. Each member must feel respected.

Questions:

1. Give reasons why leaders must maintain a professional distance from their subordinates.
2. Describe some of the different roles assumed by team members and explain how they affect the team.
3. Explain negative group behaviors and how to overcome each of them.
4. Provide examples of conflicts you have experienced in past groups and how you resolved them.
5. What are the steps required to prepare for negotiations?
6. What are the different motivational strategies that one can employ in a project team?
7. What are the five traits of successful leadership and how they impact your project team?

CHAPTER 5

Productive Global Project Teams

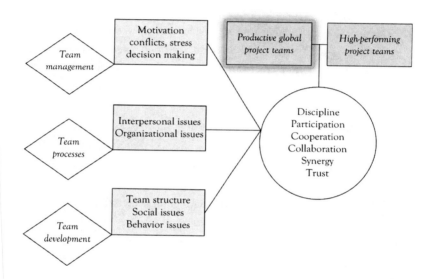

Objectives:

- Adapt management knowledge to the global scale.
- Effectively organize and utilize team members in different locations.
- Understand the advantages and disadvantages of global project teams.
- Identify differences in approaches to managing traditional and global project teams.

Preview

Chapter 5 is the logical continuation of the previous chapters. After discussing about team development processes, management of teams and leadership, the next step is to apply those skills to the global level. Global teams are often virtual in nature as they communicate and work together through the use of information systems and technology. Face-to-face communication and nonverbal communication aids are largely absent. Global project teams, although sometimes difficult to implement, provide a strategic advantage to the business. However, global projects and global project teams present unique challenges to overcome. Chapter 5 clearly explains the obstacles of political, cultural, virtual, and regional differences and how these risk characteristics need to be overcome. Due to their nature, the structure of global teams differs from that of traditional project teams. Communication, culture, and leadership assume importance in managing global projects. The chapter discussions also provide a detailed account of strengths and weaknesses of global project teams. Knowledge management and communication are key aspects of global project teams.

The convergence of information and communication technologies (ICT) and the accessibility to the consumer market all over the world in the last two decades created disappearing trade barriers and an expanding global economy. Specifically, technology has effectively decreased the size of the world in terms of increased accessibility and reach. Today, communication can be established with almost any part of the world instantly, easily, and at a low cost.

International collaborations and global projects have become attractive to companies that are seeking to expand their business horizons as these technological advances led to the creation of new markets and new customer demands, thereby alluring many aspiring organizations to join the competition. With the technological advances and productivity gains, many nations are delivering superior products and services, and seek to enter global markets. Consequently, many of the world's nations are making economic progress due to increased opportunities to participate in the global economy. Needless to say, global business is becoming more competitive.

In April 2011, Microsoft Corporation and Toyota Motor Corporation launched a strategic alliance to develop software dedicated to managing the information systems for electric vehicles for better energy management, global positioning system (GPS) systems, and multimedia technologies.[1]

The Toyota Smart Center is experimenting with a pilot program to connect people, cars, and homes for a more sustainable society. Microsoft has established other strategic collaborations to advance its communication system platforms in the automobile sector, and is hoping to expand the in-car infotainment concept, through multimedia devices, maps, social networking, and voice-activated modules to manage all of these applications.

A free-market philosophy, a technology-aided global economy, and increased international business and competition are encouraging organizations to ignore national boundaries and collaborate globally, often virtually. Technology helps people to work from anywhere; in the United States, millions work from home. People from many parts of the world participate in product design project teams for products such as smart phones, automobiles, aircrafts, pharmaceuticals, industrial machinery, and software development.

Initially started as outsourcing, international partnerships have transformed into global collaborations that led to global collaboration projects.[2] Most of these collaborations have survived based on benefits such as lowering costs, increasing revenue, and sharing technical expertise for mutual gains and technology transfer.

Global Project Teams Versus Virtual Project Teams

A global project is a transnational project with a project team consisting of individuals representing organizations from more than one country

---

[1] http://tiny.infonomia.com/
[2] MacCormack et al. (2007).

with different business cultures. Global project teams work across cultural, organizational, and national boundaries.

The ultimate global project is the International Space Station, which adds an outer space dimension to the global project team definition for enhancements and additional functionalities through discussions, meetings, troubleshooting, and other project-related activities.

A virtual team is the one that communicates electronically and team members are geographically dispersed. The geographical distance in a virtual team can vary widely. Sometimes, people from different divisions of the same organization, located in different buildings, can be part of a virtual team. Virtual teams are geographically dispersed either nationally or internationally, and any geographical distance may or may not be significant, whereas global project teams are often virtual teams where team members are dispersed geographically across national boundaries. In such cases, the geographical distance could be significant.

In other words, virtual teams can exist within an organization and in the same country for executing an internally funded project, whereas a global project employs a transnational virtual team that consists of people representing the same organization in different nations or people representing more than one organization.

Interaction and communication among the global project teams and virtual teams take place electronically. However, virtual team members tend to have a greater opportunity to meet with each other physically. The distinction between global projects and virtual teams is not straightforward. Factors such as the way information and ideas are exchanged, how knowledge is shared, and the way collaborative learning is facilitated vary based on the project type, industry type, team cultural diversity, and the number of countries participating in the project team.

Global projects are not necessarily new; they existed even before the technological advances facilitated the use of virtual teams for global projects. For example, in the manufacturing and engineering industries like automobiles, petroleum refineries, and construction, teams collaborated internationally. In these cases, different components are manufactured in different plants and places around the world, and then assembled in one central location. These collaborations started initially as outsourcing and transformed into global projects. More recently, many software development projects are executed as global projects using virtual teams, and multiple countries participate in developing and distributing several technological products that are used in our daily lives. In this example, a virtual team, with members spread globally, develops and builds a software package or a design document. However, the virtual team members may or may not be employed by the same organization.

In the service industry, where services are provided around the clock, perhaps it is possible that three separate teams in three separate global locations handle customer service that seems like 24-hour coverage. Phone services, international airlines, and Amazon are good examples of a service industry in which multiple teams in various countries work on providing service. If contacted in the morning, a response may come from someone in California. If contacted at midnight, a response may come from Singapore. These industries work on projects in a similar fashion.

In the present context, a global project is defined as the one that employs virtual teams, makes use of advances in ICT, and it is transnational. The terms *global project, global project teams, and virtual teams are all inclusive.*

Benefits of Global Project Teams

Increased competition and a global marketplace are compelling organizations to deliver products and services faster, better, and cheaper. Expertise and skilled people who can be innovative and productive are accessible globally at lower costs. Team members located in various markets are familiar with local needs and have access to knowledge specific to their location.[3] As a consequence, global projects are in vogue and global project teams are multi-organizational, multinational, multicultural, and virtual.

Global project teams provide a strategic advantage for organizations to maintain flat organization structures that facilitate easy coordination, reduce costs, increase efficiency, raise the effectiveness of workforce, and reduce delays. Eventually, coordination and communication with

---

[3] Lacerenza et al. (2015).

customers will be easier and one can achieve the coveted goal of customer satisfaction. Furthermore, global project teams can source subject matter experts from a much larger resource pool and can assemble a highly talented team that would present a wider range of perspectives. Information archiving and retrieval are easy for global project teams, an outcome and virtue of using technology-based communication.

Global project team characteristics—such as culturally diverse, geographically dispersed, and electronically communicating work groups—facilitate creativity and innovation. Furthermore, global projects are the cost-effective means by which the enterprise acquires expertise from anywhere in the world.

Global Project Teams

Global project teams can be characterized based on the level of *team virtuality*,[4] which is defined as the extent to which team members use virtual tools to coordinate and execute team processes, the amount of informational value these tools would provide, and the synchronicity of team member virtual interaction.[5]

With the advent of ICT, virtual tools are increasingly used to share project information, including the project plan, roles and responsibilities, practices, processes, daily meetings, progress data, and the like. The extent to which these technologies are used in global projects would depend on the level at which all the parties and factors (individuals, organizations, and nations) use technology routinely.

The information value of global projects would depend on the context in which these projects are executed and that context would include factors such as industry standards, practices, and policies. Global project management demands a formalized approach in the absence of informal and face-to-face communication opportunities. The documentation of practices and processes must be explicit, simple, and easy to understand.

---

[4] Miloslavic, Wildman, and Thayer (2015).
[5] Kirkman and Mathieu (2005).

Table 5.1 Virtual team factors

Extent of reliance on virtual tools:
One factor is the level of virtual interaction among team members in a virtual team. It can vary from all the interactions using virtual media to periodic interaction, task work, or both, using face-to-face without virtual tools.
Informational value:
Another factor is the value of communication sent or received through virtual tools. Rich and valuable information that is communicated varies based on the virtual tool.
Synchronicity:
A third factor is the degree to which a team's exchange of information is synchronous (in real time).

Source: Kirkman and Mathieu (2005).

Synchronicity, to a large extent, depends on the time-zone differences of the participating groups or nations in the global project, the compatibility of technology tools and the willingness of the participants to join virtual meetings, and cultural differences. Factors presented in Table 5.1 are further compounded by several other conditions that are unique to global projects, and those issues make it a challenging experience to manage global project teams.

Managing Global Projects

The lure of international collaborations and consequent global projects are attractive to organizations seeking to expand their business horizons. Collaborative networks of international partners have created new work environments that differ from the conventional business structures of the past.

A good example of international collaboration is Mercedes-Benz with Facebook. Facebook, one of the most popular social media networks, has partnered with Mercedes-Benz to develop a simplified version of the social network for drivers of the Mercedes-Benz. It is focused on locating friends and businesses. To avoid distraction from driving, the application uses basic functionality, and Facebook has provided pre-written phrases that can be published with a single push of a button.

Corning Incorporated, the world's leader in special glass and ceramics, develops and manufactures components of high-technology systems for consumer electronics, telecommunications, and life sciences. It works closely with its clients to convert ideas into products and make technological strides. Collaboration with Sharp helped Corning develop large liquid crystal display (LCD) screens. Likewise, Corning helped Verizon to deliver fast fiber-optic Internet service. Johns Hopkins University has aligned itself with Corning in the area of drug discovery.[6]

Project managers working in these new organization structures and modern multinational environments are often unprepared for the cultural, political, regional, and virtual issues that must be addressed to achieve project success.[7] From the governmental regulatory aspects of export control, foreign-exchange regulations, and international taxes to the cultural issues of work schedules, the project manager must understand and manage international obstacles and the risks associated with them.

The internal obstacles include differences in management styles, languages, ethics, and customs. Global projects are likely a departure from standard business practices, and traditional organizational structures may not be suitable to meet the complexities of project performance in the new and international project work environment. From a risk management perspective, the characteristics of global projects that must be understood and managed are listed in Table 5.2.

Table 5.2 provides an overview of the potential threats of a collaborative international project. One must recognize that each global project is unique and the lists of potential risks identified in the table serve as reference only and provide a starting point. Unique risks may exist for each project, and the selected project should be further analyzed and reviewed in detail.

---

[6] Turiera and Cros (2013).
[7] Steffey and Anantatmula (2011).

Table 5.2 Risk characteristics of global projects

Cultural	Political
• Native language; number of languages on the project • Cultural values • Different currencies • Work ethics • Religion • Teamwork versus individual effort • Trust • Dispute management • Standards terminology and differing priorities • Management practices and expertise • Economic culture • Inflation • Market conditions • Interest rates • Exchange rates	• Terrorism • Firm's relationship to government • Prior working relationships • Revolution/civil wars • Government's desire for project • Relationship with local activist and power groups (environmental, labor unions) • Use of local businesses • Relations with neighboring countries • Laws and regulations • Environmental compliance • National views toward firm • Tax composition • Import/export control • Expropriation/seizure/espionage
Virtual	**Regional**
• Time-zone differences • Communication issues • Number of geographic locations • Number of business organizations and teams • Past team experiences • Management experience • Clear understanding of scope among parties • Organizational structures • Roles and responsibilities	• Local (crime, vandalism, corruption, theft, bribery) • Safety issues • Resource availability and quality • Skilled work force • Technology limitations • Climate and weather • Familiarity with region • Geological conditions • Environmental impacts • Housing availability • Transportation • Demonstrations, riots

Source: Steffey and Anantatmula (2011).

Challenges in Managing Global Project Teams

Team and Culture Diversity

As is true with any project team, global project teams are also temporary. Team members, by definition, generally have no common history and it is not easy to have team cohesion for this reason alone. This challenge is compounded by the fact that the team members represent varying work cultures, languages, business ethics and values, professionalism, and attitudes toward work. Consequently, the team is expected to have differing attitudes toward work, hierarchy, delegation, authority, accountability, and responsibility. A team charter helps to address many of these issues. The importance of the team charter is discussed in the next chapter.

Absence of Informal Communications

One cannot overestimate the value and contribution of informal interactions and the crucial role informal networks play in traditional and colocated teams. However, informal interactions and social networks are largely absent in global project teams. Even if present, social interactions and networks tend to be ineffective. Likewise, face-to-face interactions in formal and informal gatherings and meetings are very useful in building team cohesion and a common understanding of the work at hand. On the contrary, global and virtual project team interactions, facilitated by tools and technology, often are task focused and mechanistic. Therefore, managing global project teams exacerbates the complexity that is inherent for any global project.

Managing Conflicts

The absence of face-to-face and nonverbal communication makes it difficult to recognize the existence of a conflict, let alone the resolution of it. Furthermore, various cultures in the world deal with conflict differently. People from low-context cultures like Holland, Australia, Canada, and the United States may like to confront and address the conflict overtly. However, people from high-context culture societies like Japan and China may not be willing to discuss a conflict openly. As the project manager, formal and clearly defined processes need to be instituted that deal with management philosophy, work-related policies, management practices, and procedures to minimize incidences of conflict.

Research[8] shows that collaborative conflict management, and a high concern for self and others in integrating opposing views, is considered

---

[8] Montoya-Weiss, Massey, and Song (2001); Paul et al. (2004); Scott and Wildman (2015).

effective for global virtual teams as compared to other conflict management strategies such as *avoidance, accommodation,* or *compromising.* Spontaneous communication and a common understanding among team members are considered effective in managing conflict. Conflict, to a certain extent, is desirable in decision making, however.

Unfamiliarity and Difference

The global project team is associated with unfamiliarity and global project leadership requires additional competencies beyond those that are necessary to manage traditional teams. As the project manager, one must have understanding and competency in managing different cultures that are integral to the global project team. Furthermore, it is desirable to develop knowledge about the leadership styles that are best suited to representing regions and nations. As the global project manager, there is a need to develop:

- Competency in managing multi-cultures
- Knowledge of leadership styles expected by different regions and nations
- Awareness of team members' interpersonal and nonverbal cues
- Adaptability to different cultures, practices, and expectations
- Ability to manage technical demands and information overload
- Ability to manage multiple differences inherent in a global project team

It is very important to establish leadership and adapt one's directive leadership style during the initial stages of a global project to counter challenges associated with unfamiliarity among the team members and diverse cultures and work practices. The initial leadership style should preferably be directive and not supportive during the initial phases of the project.

In Chapter 2, we discussed the *same* and *difference* issues and their impact on developing and managing teams. People have the propensity to categorize other people and things into either *same* or *different.* In general, people look for and align with people of similar age group, same language, and the same geographical location. Likewise, there is an innate tendency to interpret unfamiliarity (*difference*) as a threat and it can lead to a chain reaction of negative biases, attitudes, and behaviors. This presents a challenge in managing global project teams where diversity and *differences* assume importance in team performance and learning.

Research[9] has shown that our brains recognize only the *difference* (not the culture) and it creates negative bias, competition, withdrawal, and distrust among the team members. However, a competent project leader is generally aware of these potential biases and knows how to control them. As a successful global project team leader, one should recognize the *difference* and must be well versed with managing the *difference*.

In general, virtual team members do not share mental models that reflect similar or common knowledge and understanding. Beliefs that contribute to team performance are not shared among the team members. Furthermore, it is difficult to establish trust among the team members due to their heavy reliance on technology for communication, which is often formal, mechanistic, and task oriented. Building trust is important, and a high level of trust among team members improves collaboration and team performance. It is contingent upon the team leader to recognize these deficiencies in the team and to work toward team efficacy.

Structure of Global Project Teams

The team structure of global projects would largely depend on the project size, project complexity, number of countries and cultures it represents, team size, extent of geographical dispersion, and project duration.

1. *High interdependence* places emphasis on relations in virtual teams and demands greater communication using communication-friendly technologies such as videoconferencing. These technologies mimic communications in traditional and colocated teams. Also, higher interdependence is likely to encourage open communication that leads to collaboration and cohesion.

---

[9] Wildman and Griffith (2015).

2. *Role structure* is aimed at defining the roles of individuals and reducing role conflict and ambiguity. If a project's scope is complex or if it is associated with unknowns and uncertainties, it is important to define roles clearly, specifically in global project teams due to communication challenges. Both functional and divisional role structures would work well in global projects.

3. *Leadership structure* would depend on the project size and project team size, and shared leadership may be preferred for mega projects. Shared leadership for global project teams leads to better team effectiveness and higher performance.

4. *Communication structure.* Information sharing takes place between two individuals or in groups through formal meetings or informal networks. Furthermore, communication can be formal (reports) and informal (within the project team). The absence of nonverbal communication and dependence on technology compel virtual teams to have formal, structured, and open communication systems to increase effectiveness. Global project teams face other communication challenges such as trust, differences in culture, and knowledge-sharing restrictions.

5. *Physical dispersion* is characterized by the number of locations and the number of people in each location. Multiple locations across national boundaries present greater challenges to global virtual teams due to social, political, legal, philosophical, and other cultural differences.

6. *Team duration* is specific and ad hoc for projects. However, global projects with longer durations will have an opportunity to develop a common understanding as compared to projects with short duration. With the awareness of working together for a long period, project team members enjoy greater synergy after initial phases. On the other hand, the longer the project duration, the greater the need for well-developed processes and practices as project teams are likely to experience turnover.

To sum up, the project manager must consider all the aforementioned variables before devising the project team structure. When the global project duration is long, formal processes and a formal and well-developed communication structure are important. The project manager must consider using interactive tools such as videoconferencing to have informal and social times. Similarly, if the physical dispersion is large and many country locations and people are included in the project team, it is a good idea to consider shared leadership; to delegate responsibilities; to build competencies within the team to deal with cultural diversity; to make use of advanced interactive tools; and to place greater emphasis on communication, specifically about project execution, monitoring, and controlling.

Furthermore, organizations are compelled to recognize the need to educate and enhance the technical knowledge and skills of their workforce due to rapid advances in ICT coupled with increasing competition. ICT is changing the way traditional and virtual teams communicate and a wide range of technologies and communication methods are available to choose from. However, often these technologies might lead to information overload. Both the extremes—information overload and lack of information—are not acceptable.

Knowledge Sharing in Global Projects

The global economy is impacting the way organizations manage their institutional knowledge. It necessitated a departure from standard business practices and traditional organizational structures. Sharing information and knowledge has become indispensable for organizations to manage international collaborations and global projects effectively. It helps participating organizations to learn from each other.

However, a downside of global projects is that certain organizational knowledge that is proprietary—a critical resource that competitors cannot easily replicate and the basis for sustaining competitive advantage—is no longer confined within organizations. Thus, it becomes a challenge to retain the competitive edge of organizations while participating in global projects. Organizations will have to make the distinction between the core competitive knowledge that needs to be retained within and other relevant knowledge that is necessary to share for effective collaboration and the successful completion of global projects. Furthermore, working conditions and communication systems of global project teams exacerbate an individual's lack of willingness to share knowledge.

There are many other issues that hinder knowledge sharing in global project teams. The very reasons that are considered beneficial to use a virtual team could lead to obstacles; temporarily assigned members of global project teams typically come from different national, ethnic, functional, and educational backgrounds, reside in different countries or continents with different time zones, and rarely or never see each other in person. Generally, there is no interest in sharing their knowledge.

Informal and extemporaneous information exchange among team members and socialization aid in facilitating the creation of new ideas and sharing of these ideas and knowledge. However, spontaneous information exchange and socialization are difficult in global project teams. Also, team members are often separated by different time zones, which preclude synchronous and real-time collaboration. Generational differences and attitudes compound the communication problem further.

Cultural diversity is a norm in global project teams; knowledge and related terms have different meanings in different cultures. Research shows that the cultural identity of individuals is inextricably tied to their native language and individuals still have a strong preference for conducting business in their native language. The idea of what constitutes a good performance and accountability can vary among different cultures and this could lead to project risk and failure.

The absence of learning opportunities, such as social networking and informal information exchange, is prompting global project managers to encourage knowledge sharing that is tied to improved project performance by creating incentives for project team members for collaborative learning. While creating these incentives, one needs to be mindful of the fact that incentives are culture specific as the perceived value of proprietary knowledge varies from culture to culture. For instance, recognition is valued more in certain societies as compared to monetary benefits. Furthermore, these incentives must outweigh the perceived value of knowledge so that benefits are accrued to improve the project performance.

Critical Factors of Global Project Teams

An extensive study of global projects identified several significant factors that influence global project performance and success. These can be classified as internal (Table 5.3) and external (Table 5.4) to the global project team.

Table 5.3 Global project team—external factors

Factor	Description
Global business environment	An understanding of all the global business environmental issues including international market, the global economy, international finance, and currency will influence decision making.
Legal and political issues	Country-specific laws, environmental regulations, political issues, and acceptable standards can impact a global project.
Global procurement	Procurement will have no geographical boundaries. Therefore, it is a challenge to possess the knowledge of the best places to go for materials and labor, which can impact global project success.
Stakeholder and customer satisfaction	Cultural, financial, and communication complications can occur in terms of determining what the customer considers a successful project.
Time-zone differences	Time-zone differences can create communication (meetings) problems, specifically in a synchronous mode. However, time-zone differences can also allow work to proceed 24 hours a day.
Cultural values	Religion and beliefs will have impact on a project in terms of work ethics, values, holidays, who will work with whom, and work practices. Local, regional, and national business and management practices vary and could be different from Western norms, such as time off from work, hierarchical authority, and gender issues.

Table 5.4 Global project team—internal factors

Factor	Description
Leadership and trust	Leadership and people skills are more important for global projects. Suck skills help in establishing trust. Micromanaging is a temptation in global projects due to the absence of nonverbal communication, a lack of understanding of the capabilities of the project team members including contractors, and the absence of trust.
Fast and reliable information systems	Fast and reliable information systems are essential for success in global projects. Communication and control systems that are standard, compatible, and reliable are essential for knowledge sharing.
Project organization and structure	Cost-effective organization structure that is decentralized and flexible is necessary to collaborate and manage global projects successfully to meet customer needs.
Integration management	Vertical (within the organization) and horizontal integration (external organization) are critical and can become difficult across regions and countries.

Compared to project managers managing traditional projects, project managers managing global projects are required to have more knowledge about cost management; have the ability to lead diverse global project teams; and must have the understanding of international, technical, and human factors of project management. Factors listed in the Tables 5.3 and 5.4 underline the importance of the leadership role in managing global projects.

Culture, communication, and leadership assume importance in either fostering or hampering team performance in global projects. If a diverse culture is not managed well or the right leadership is not provided, managers would impact communication effectiveness within the team that can lead to conflicts among team members.

Communication

It is an established fact that communication is a critical factor for project success and project team performance. Challenges associated with cultural differences and formal communication approaches would negatively impact the recognition of conflicts and conflict resolutions. Furthermore, asynchronous communication, often used by global project teams, may result in prolonged discussions without coming to an agreement or understanding in making a decision.

Global project teams rely heavily on electronic media to communicate. The nonverbal aspect of communication, which plays an important role in communications, is literally absent. Furthermore, each individual creates the context while receiving a message and the context would depend on our past experience, insights, knowledge, and history with the sender in addition to the message itself. The ability to expand this context would be vastly increased in face-to-face communication. The notion that *if you can be misunderstood, you will be*, happens more often in global projects.

By definition, communication challenges are associated with not understanding or sharing affective, cognitive, or perceptual meanings. The following factors are identified to improve communication effectiveness in global project teams:[10]

---

[10] Scott and Wildman (2015).

- Frequency of communication
- Depth of communication
- Videoconferencing
- Open communication channels and participation
- Building relationships and trust
- Respect for cultures and languages
- Check for mutual understanding of tasks
- Building group identity

Communication challenges, including the absence of nonverbal communication, and cross-cultural issues also inhibit efforts in establishing trust in virtual teams. Research has shown that geographical dispersion and cultural diversity act as barriers to communication effectiveness and contribute to conflict as well.

Culture

Research has shown that diversity among team members, as a result of differences represented by national and local cultures, is likely to cause misunderstandings and distrust, thereby increasing the incidence of conflict. Cross-cultural training to develop cultural sensitivity, informal and social opportunities to understand and appreciate cultural differences, and an appreciation for the value of diversity would help in leveraging the value of diversity in global project teams.

Leadership

Often, global projects have the advantage of recruiting innovative and productive people internationally, who possess the requisite expertise and skills at lower costs. Global project teams, therefore, tend to be comprised of experts from around the world, known for their unique ability to address project complexity. The leadership of global projects is becoming more about facilitating and supporting. For the same reasons, shared and distributed leadership works well for global project teams. Emotional intelligence, empathy, and appreciation for diversity can help a global project manager to succeed. It is worth repeating that directive leadership and establishing authority during the initial stages of the project are important to set direction and eliminate negative emotions among the team members who deal with unfamiliarity.

Managing Global Projects Successfully

In a study[11] of global projects and project managers, a model for managing global projects successfully was developed after identifying key performance factors and relationships among these factors (Figure 5.1). The arrow in the figure should be read as "leads to."

Figure 5.1 shows that culture is the independent variable and influences the leadership style and resultant trust that is established among the project team members. Leadership style must adapt to the prevailing cultures and the cultural differences that are present in the project environment.

It is logical that cultural factors also dictate the adoptability of technology and influence the design of the information system such as level of sophistication, types of information tools, and communication techniques. Once installed, it is important to maintain and upgrade the information system to ensure its performance at the desired speed and reliability levels throughout the project management life cycle.

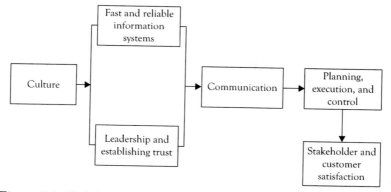

Figure 5.1 Global project success model

---

[11] Anantatmula and Thomas (2010).

One's leadership style must adapt to the prevailing cultures and the cultural differences that are present in the project environment. Leadership and resultant trust help create effective communication that must be sustained throughout the project life. All these factors together must precede management of the core project management phases, including project planning, project execution, and control to achieve stakeholder and customer satisfaction.

Geographically dispersed project teams that do not have an opportunity to get the project status experience lower levels of motivation. Understanding the cultural differences, engaging leadership, building trust, and communicating effectively would help to avoid such pitfalls.

It should be remembered, however, that the importance and impact of some of the factors that contribute to performance of global projects are industry specific. Depending on the type of industry in which the project is executed, the relative importance of these factors may vary.

Differences in Managing Traditional and Global Projects

In traditional projects, the selection of project teams and assigning roles are important first steps, whereas in global project projects, it is important to establish leadership and design information systems first.

In traditional, colocated projects, the initial steps are selecting the team, defining roles and responsibilities, employing consistent processes, and communicating expectations. Likewise, studies on project success identified success factors such as clearly defined goals, adequate communication with all of the stakeholders including the project team, and the ability to handle unexpected problems.

However, in global projects, which are routinely managed with virtual teams and diverse cultures, the establishment of leadership and trust that is sensitive to the culture in context is the initial step and assumes importance during the early phases of the project, before initiating core project management activities. Establishing leadership and information systems in the initial phases of the project life cycle exerts significant influence on the project success in a global environment.

Desirable Attributes of Global Project Virtual Teams

The success of a global project team would be enhanced if the team members were suited for virtual work because of their personalities and personal preferences. There are several comprehensive personality instruments that would test the compatibility of a prospective team member with the virtual environment.

It is commonly believed that most people are either readers or listeners, in that there is a preference to read project material, or have a person describe the content to them. In this simple example, the readers are more suited to virtual teams.

It can be determined if the prospective team member gets an emotional and intellectual charge from being with people and from being recognized in public settings, or if the prospect derives more personal satisfaction from individual accomplishments, and with minimal fanfare, although the accomplishment needs to be recognized nonetheless. Again, the latter person would be more suited to work on a virtual team. Other tests would be to pose questions such as the following:

- Traditional team candidate
  - *Do you need face-to-face social interaction during the conduct of the project?*
  - *Do you have to use body language and tone of voice to express yourself?*
  - *Do you need a boss/coworker to keep an eye on you to stay on task?*
  - *Do you need to physically or visually represent your thoughts?*
  - *Do you need to be micromanaged and/or micromanage others?*
  - *Do you have problems staying focused when not in a traditional office setting?*
  - *Is physically connecting with team members necessary to you for team-building purposes?*
  - *Are face-to-face meetings necessary to discuss project specifics?*

- Virtual team candidate
  - *Are you able to effectively express yourself in text form?*
  - *Are you able to effectively communicate with persons or a team which you have never met before?*
  - *Do you feel comfortable and capable when conveying your thoughts, reports, and presentations via the web or some other virtual venue?*
  - *Are you more successful working independently?*

If the response to most of the first set of questions is *no*, then the person is probably compatible with the virtual team environment. Likewise, if the response to most of the second set of questions is *yes*, then the person is probably compatible with the virtual team environment.

Essentially, most of the virtual team issues can be handled by introducing a high level of formality of procedures and the general personality disposition of the team members. Given that formality of project management is far more important in virtual teams, and given that sophisticated organizations have formalized their project management processes, the difference between traditional and virtual teams is insignificant in sophisticated organizations.

One of the most interesting examples of a pure virtual environment is the work between air traffic controllers and airplane pilots. Although these individuals will probably never meet in person, their relationship has been formalized such that each person knows how to ask for information, how to ask for action, and how to respond to both, in the most cordial fashion. The cordiality is often intertwined with a certain degree of trust that is present in the relationship.

Questions:

1. Explain how global project teams provide advantages to businesses.
2. Describe the differences between virtual project teams and global project teams.
3. List three strengths and weaknesses of global project teams.

4. Provide an example of a global project team and some of the risk characteristics that the team faces.

5. Differentiate communication process between traditional and global project teams.

6. What are the challenges associated with global project teams with respect to cultural differences?

CHAPTER 6

High Performing Project Teams

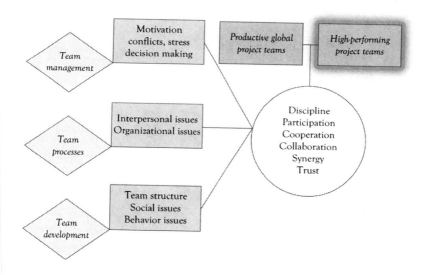

Objectives:

- Recognize the traits of successful teams.
- Utilize metrics to track and improve team performance.
- Learn how to enhance team cohesion.
- Understand the characteristics of effective project teams.
- Recognize important processes of project teams to improve their performance.

Preview

Team performance can be measured in terms of psychosocial and task outcomes. Effective teams, although pursuing different goals, often exhibit many of the same traits, such as interdependency, trust, and communication. Teams are strongly influenced by the organizational culture. These mind-sets and paradigms stem from upper management and permeate down into all facets of the organization. Organizational culture can be seen in the development of a project team charter, which lays out the goals and structure of the team, desirable performance attributes, and behavioral expectations. Performance guidelines and metrics may also be included in the team charter, or team members could be informed at a later time. Team cohesion and performance strongly depend on individual team members adhering to the behavioral code of conduct. Team cohesion is especially vital in global project teams, and due to their virtual nature, it is optimal for all team members to closely follow the leader's guidelines and directives.[1]

Team work divides the task and multiplies success
—Unknown

Teams are formed to help organizations deliver products, services, and improve their quality, productivity, and profits. Teams are also expected to facilitate better decision making, and improve organizational processes and practices. Working in teams has benefits from an individual perspective; work satisfaction, knowledge, and quality of work life are likely to improve. Furthermore, work teams share problems and find solutions together, support each other in completing tasks, make decisions collectively, and resolve conflicts. While doing so, trust is gradually established among the team members, and with the leader. Building trust is one of the most important aspects of a team.

Team performance is classified into two broad areas: task outcomes and psychosocial outcomes.[2]

- *Task outcomes* denote meeting the estimated schedule and budget.

---

[1] Part of this chapter is adopted from *Successful Project Management Practices* by Rad and Anantatmula (2010).
[2] Pinto and Pinto (1990).

- *Psychosocial outcomes* suggest the degree of experienced friendliness and support among team members.

In a similar vein, project teams are formed with a primary purpose to deliver project outcomes within cost and time (task-related functions) and it is possible only when team members work together with collaboration and support (people-related functions). Both are important for synergy and success in project teams.

Simply bringing people together as a team does not produce these desired outcomes. Instead, managers must help develop teams and avoid or eliminate inhibitors through collective leadership, reward systems, team structure and membership, and group processes. People who have been members of poorly performing teams are well aware of the shortcomings when team-development issues are not addressed.

The literature[3] suggests that effective teams: (1) are interdependent, (2) are more efficient working together than individually, (3) function well to create their own magnetism, (4) do not always have the same leader, (5) care and nurture one another, (6) cheer for the leader, who—in turn—cheers them, and (7) have a high level of trust.

Although teams are expected to improve performance, one should be vigilant about signs of ineffectiveness and take prompt action. Some of the indicators for immediate attention are complaints, grievances, and low morale among team members, people-focused conflicts, unclear work assignments, lack of commitment and initiation, lack of coordination, low trust, and perceived unfairness in reward systems. Specifically, the need for team building is recognized when team meetings are ineffective and are seen as a waste of time.

Organization Culture

Every organization will take on a culture with the passage of time. The most important factors in the behavior of the team are the enterprise culture and the personality of the team members as team-specific people

---

[3] Whetten and Cameron (2011).

issues are partly dependent on the culture of the enterprise, and less on the project's or team's mission.

The culture of an organization is somewhat akin to the personality of an individual. The organization culture is more powerful and more pervasive than the culture that the team might adopt or develop. As a result, senior management must be careful as to the kind of subtle messages that it sends to its employees with respect to people issues. The team culture would also depend on whether the team manages a project, a portfolio, or a proposal.

Building an organization culture starts with defining a policy on performance standards and behavioral norms. Operationalizing these standards and norms starts with recruitment. Defining these standards and norms should be done during the initial stages of starting an organization followed by recruitment of like-minded people who are likely to cherish and promote these standards and norms. Many examples of such organizations are found everywhere in the world.

One should be mindful that once an organizational culture is in place, it is not easy to change. The challenge is to get rid of undesirable norms and standards and replace them with newer ones as organizations evolve. Managing changes in organizational culture resonates with managing projects as well. On the other hand, change is inevitable for projects. Evolving organizational culture and advances in project management practices mutually influence each other in bringing changes to practices, standards, and norms. A recent study[4] found that organizations with highly effective communication and change management practices are more than twice as likely to outperform those organizations that are not effective in either of these areas.

Delegation Versus Micromanagement

Probably one of the most common forms of organizational structure is that of hierarchical, and the same structure is translated to project team structures in those organizations. Frequently, this form of enterprise management is blended with micromanagement. This characteristic hands-on

---

[4] Towers Watson (2014).

form of management by the senior management is a definite advantage during the periods that the organization is in its infancy. However, as the enterprise grows, this form of management should be abandoned in favor of one that is suitable for a larger enterprise. The same holds true for projects and project teams.

From the project management perspective, a micromanagement mode of enterprise management will stifle creativity of the project team members. This form of management places the burden of innovations and day-to-day problem solving directly on the proverbial shoulder of the project lead or senior management. Thus, the team members will be forced to a position of either asking senior management what should be done in the face of an emerging situation or, worse yet, waiting to be told what to do.

Mature organizations adopt the delegation mode of operation and will allow the staff to become creative, innovative, and fully responsive to the emerging problems of projects. In a creativity-based project management environment, which is the delegation management style, the team members will either recommend and then take action or, better yet, solve the problem and then advise the project manager and senior management of the novel solution that remedied that emerging problem.

A manifestation of the existence of micromanagement, and lack of confidence, is the multisignature approval processes for project initiation, and for major project decisions. The multisignature process refers to the typical process by which the original plan, and the subsequent changes to that plan, of the project will be processed by the team members. It is typical that a project document will have to be approved by several levels of management, as signified by as many signatures on the approval sheet, before the document is considered to have been authorized. An interesting side effect of this multisignature process is that the credit is shared, but so is the accountability.

The issues of micromanagement and trust, or lack thereof, are closely tied to each other. Mature organizations develop confidence in project managers and project teams. If and when this hierarchical approval process were to be eliminated, or at least tempered, it would provide symbolic evidence that the senior management trusts the judgment of, and appreciates the sacrifices of, the project team.

The increase in outsourcing and the increase in the use of global projects, in both internally funded and externally funded projects, have provided a more widespread use for the delegation concept. Delegation of authority to the project team is one of the major foundation items for sophistication in project management because it signals the presence of support and trust attributes.

Delegation comes with authority and accountability. The senior management of the organization must extend the authority for the implementation of the project to the project manager and the team and hold them accountable for the success of the project. The project team should be directly responsible for the success of the project through detailed planning, skillful execution, and tactful scope change management. In such an environment, project team members would be empowered to take innovative actions to solve emerging project problems and to conduct continuous improvement in project processes. The prerequisite for this process is that the senior management must create an environment conducive to loyalty, self-sufficiency, and trust.

High-Performing Project Management Teams

By definition, projects are associated with uncertainties and unknowns and these two factors vary from project to project. It is reasonable to assume that, in project management, the issue is not if the plan will change, rather it is when or what will change, and by how much. The importance of the project manager's leadership will be heighted during the frequent occasions when there are significant changes to the project mission.

In a mature and well-managed enterprise, there can be three different types of teams engaged in project management activities: a project team, a proposal team, and a portfolio team (Table 6.1).

The success of the project team will be judged based on the measurable values of scope, cost, and duration. The success of the proposal team has two components: drafting a winning proposal and the subsequent profit from the ensuing project. The success of the portfolio team is measured by the attributes of the projects or proposals that are considered to be the most appropriate for the prevailing strategic and financial direction of the enterprise.

Table 6.1 Types of teams

Project team	Project team success measures
• Exclusively for managing a project • Time bound • Transient teams • Assembly of multiple skills and expertise • Work under the constraints of time, cost, scope, and quality	• Completion of project within time • Completion of project within cost • Meeting project delivery outcomes (scope and quality) • Satisfy key stakeholders including the client and end-user • Contributing to project management maturity • Build competencies of project team members
Proposal team	**Proposal team success measures**
• Meant for writing several proposals • Relatively a permanent team • Less transient teams • Assembly of multiple skills • Work under the constraint of time	• Drafting a winning proposal • Increasing the proposal win rate • Identifying proposal that make best use of existing resources • Increasing the revenue • Diversifying the portfolio and aligning with strategic goals
Portfolio team	**Portfolio team success measures**
• Meant for managing portfolio of projects • Long-term responsibilities • Strategic team • Finance, policy, and strategic skills • Work under the constraints of optimum use of resources and finances	• Stream of projects aligned with strategic goals • Stream of proposals aligned with strategic goals • Long-term success of the organization • Increased market share • Increased profit • Expansion of business

The success of each team is measured by the outcome of the desired attributes of the respective deliverable of the team. Additionally, enlightened organizations pay special attention to the people attributes of teams, with the presumption that fostering harmonious teamwork favorably impacts the performance of the teams in subtle but significant ways. The project manager plays an important role as a leader and manager to foster and encourage synergy.

A successful project manager is expected to possess competencies and skills such as situational leadership skills; emotional intelligence; effective communication skills; savvy at organizational politics; and a clear understanding of the vision, values, and beliefs. Team management is considered an important competence for managing projects successfully. Furthermore, the project manager must be capable of multitasking, problem solving, and decision making.

Team Attributes

Project team attributes would include performance norms such as the level of effort, reporting, and punctuality. Moreover, team attributes should include the manner in which the members of the team relate to each other and cooperate with each other, toward their unified mission. Thus important behavioral norms include communication and conflict management. Most importantly, the team attributes highlight the extent to which the team possesses the subtle but desirable attributes of dedication, commitment to a unified goal, team spirit, harmony, and trust.

Probably one of the most effective means of assuring the repeatable success of a team is to provide guidelines for accomplishing the mission of the team. The key is to replace the ad hoc norms with detailed and formal norms, processes, and tools. One of the beneficial aspects of formalization of the team is that it will streamline the process by which the enterprise would recognize, promote, and reward that illusive concept known as team spirit.

Articulation of the ultimate goals of the team and formalization of the means by which those goals will be achieved are the fundamentals of managing the attributes of projects. Well-defined and mature enterprise processes and guidelines for planning and managing project cost, time, and scope would facilitate the formalization of professional performance. Likewise, formalization of the personal interactions among team members, with the assistance of enterprise guidelines, will clarify the conduct of the personal interactions.

Team Charter

Group norms are either written or unwritten rules that govern the behavior of team members. These norms include but are not limited to work ethic, honesty, integrity, respect, conflict management, decision making,

Table 6.2 Team charter

Basic performance	Specify
• Reporting processes • Elemental data reporting • Responsibilities and assignments • Set consequences of nonconformance • Timeliness (attendance and delivery) • Work hours	• Time spent • Obligations • Reporting • Deliverables • Knowledge sharing • Tracking (plan versus actual)
Personal behavior expectations	**Attitudinal expectations**
• Civility • Meeting protocols • Social graces • Decision protocol • Receiving/offering assistance	• Cooperative stance • Honest communication • Conflict recognition • Negotiations • Teamwork
Desirable norms	**Expected outcomes**
• Demeanor • Communication • Conflict management • Negotiation	• Trust • Team spirit • Harmony • Cohesiveness • Rare major conflicts • Commitment

and communication protocols. A preferred practice is developing a team charter to define these norms for common understanding and agreement (Table 6.2).

The team charter is the instrument by which the enterprise documents and describes how the team members are expected to collaborate in the activities of the project, participate in making decisions, and more importantly how team members work in concert with one another. The team charter would specify professional performance and the personal behavior of the team members with a hopeful expectation of achieving positive harmony, teamwork, team spirit, and dedication.

Typically, a team charter begins by defining specific performance expectations, such as timeliness in delivering promised outputs, e-mail etiquette, and phone protocol. Equally important, the team charter will then highlight the standards for behaving as members of a unified and cohesive team in the difficult-to-define areas of communication, cooperation, conflict management, and civility. The unspoken and unspecified hope of the team charter is that it will invoke the desired team facets such as trust, respect, and commitment.

There is a relationship between the project charter and the team charter in that the team charter will describe the means of achieving the project charter. The shorthand description of this concept would be that the project charter specifies the deliverable by responding to the question of "what is to be accomplished," whereas the team charter specifies the response to "how will it be accomplished."

Team Charter
Team charter is primarily developed to provide direction for both explicit and implicit behaviors, attitudes, and responsibilities of the team members to achieve its purpose. It includes some of the norms for working together as a team and what the expected behavioral and attitudinal outcomes should be. The team leader and the team members create this document, which serves as a roadmap.

The format and content of the team charter vary depending on the team type (virtual or traditional), team size, project complexity, and constraints with which the team has to perform.

Communication norms and organizational culture influence the effectiveness of a team charter and all three of them must be aligned for optimum results. Abiding to the team charter is likely to establish trust, improve team spirit, cohesiveness, and reduce incidence of conflicts.

The team charter should include processes and guidelines for developing patterns of cooperative and communicative behavior, procedures for determining signs of conflict, guidelines for recognizing conflict, and procedures for mitigating or resolving conflict. An expected outcome of the charter is that the conflict-management processes will be used less and less, because intellectual diversity will be resolved at the minor levels, as part of the organizational culture, and not by using formalized tools for communication and collegial debate.

The spirit of the team charter should become topics of the orientation for new internal transfers to any of the project management functions.

Thus, new employees will be informed of and trained in the intricacies of managing specific team performance attributes, people interaction attributes, and attitudinal attributes of the team. Such an orientation process for the new team members will help those who come into the enterprise from other possibly unsophisticated enterprises. Finally, the essence of the team charter should become a guideline during the external hiring process of new employees into the organization.

People-related policies contained in the team charter on an organization-wide basis will hopefully result in a corporate culture that is friendly to projects and conducive to success of those projects. If the same team is commissioned to work on another project, the preparation of a team charter will be far simpler. The professional performance and technical duties might be modified slightly although the personal and behavioral instructions and the attitudinal expectations will stay unchanged.

Professional Performance Guidelines

The professional performance part of the team charter addresses the team's activities such as identifying specific tasks or deliverables and responsibilities of each team member and the manner in which the deliverable will be accomplished. Behavioral interactions and attitudinal issues of the team members influence the results of the team members' professional performance actions.

This part of the team charter will specify the project work breakdown structure (WBS) components, and the team members to whom each component has been assigned. Then, the specific details for project planning, execution, monitoring, control, and closeout of the project will be addressed, particularly as related to the project and to the project team. It will outline the responsibility of each team member and the team as a whole in the areas of cost, duration, scope/quality, and risk.

A team member might be assigned to several components. Conversely, a component might require the efforts of several team members. If more than one person is assigned to a component, one person would be assigned as the lead person.

The details to be addressed here are what to report, how to report, and when to report. For example, items to be reported, through logging into the project-reporting portal every Wednesday, could be effort spent, effort needed, and expected delivery. Additional performance details include deadlines for component delivery, durations of meetings, and presentations.

Prescribed Behavior

The personal behavior part of the team charter will prescribe the details of behavioral guidelines as to how to handle communication, conflict, and negotiations. This part of the charter would include a code of conduct, which should become a reference document throughout the project. The unspoken, but clearly hoped, expectation is that, in time, the team would operate with the utmost amount of harmony, trust, teamwork, and dedication.

Behavioral attributes describe the human dynamics of the team. This portion of the team charter will describe modes and manners in which the behavioral attributes are handled, acknowledging the fact that the collective behavior of team members will have a major impact on the attitudinal attributes of the team members and on the success in the professional performance areas. By comparison, professional performance refers to an individual responsibility and to some extent the dry and formal side of teamwork.

In a way, the intent of the team charter is to mandate team performance and recommend personal behavior and then measure the results of that performance through team professional productivity and project success. The presumption is that it is precisely the immeasurable attitudinal attributes of respect and teamwork that are at the core of a team's success.

Productive Project Team—Stages of Development

People are motivated by challenges and opportunities to further their career goals. Those who are assigned to project teams are almost always interested in accomplishing personal and professional goals in addition to completing their project responsibilities. Project managers should understand the personal aspirations of their project team members and support them in their aspirations. As leaders, project managers play an important role in motivating and guiding people to simultaneously complete project responsibilities and grow as professionals.

Team Formation and Introduction

Team formation occurs during the project initiation stage. Whenever feasible, the project manager should play an important role in team selection. Team members are identified and selected based on required skills for project tasks and the likelihood of making a contribution to the successful completion of the project. Defining roles and responsibilities based on the strengths and skills of team members and clearly communicating what is expected are the critical initial steps in developing an effective project team.

Team Conflict

Differences in personality types, motivation, personal and professional goals, levels of expertise, cultural differences, and levels of commitment often influence and give rise to conflicts among the team members. The project manager must pay attention to early signs of conflicts and disagreements that are manifested both in verbal and nonverbal forms and must resolve them promptly during the project initiation and planning phases. A directive leadership style in controlling negative emotions and conflict management strategies are important during the early stages of a conflict and during the initial stages of project team development.

Team Cohesion

Communication clarity in negotiating roles, responsibilities, and expected deliverables of each and every individual of the team, to a great extent, would reduce conflict and increase cohesion. The team charter plays a critical role in defining behavioral norms, respect, civility, and courtesy during daily interactions and communications. One cannot overestimate their role in building team cohesion. Informal social gatherings and happy hours would speed up team development and cohesion.

Team Performance

Ideally, project teams perform efficiently and effectively during the later stages of the planning and execution phases after going through initial challenges. The project manager plays a supportive role and maintains harmony. It is important to notice conflict or potential conflict at the initial stages and address it promptly. Communication about progress monitoring and sharing encouraging progress data would motivate people to perform better. A good project manager learns to take the blame if things go wrong and gives credit to team members for the team's accomplishments.

Team Diffusion

As the project nears completion, the project manager must plan for the transition of team members to other assignments and projects (or new responsibilities) with a focus on continuing support for personal and professional goals of each and every team member. It is preferable to hold back appreciation, recognition, and the reward of a team member until the project is complete. The project manager must provide fair and honest feedback to each team member to recognize their strengths and identify areas for improvement and make every effort to develop their abilities.

Importance of Communication and Reporting

Communication and reporting are often used interchangeably. However, they are different. Reporting refers to the transfer of formal and factual information to key stakeholders within and outside the organization on the project performance issues such as cost, schedule, risk, scope, and quality. On the other hand, communication signifies the informal transfer of information between the individuals within the organization and usually deals with the subjects of behavior and personal interaction. Compared to reporting, which is a formal, planned, and scheduled event, communication is spontaneous and unplanned (Table 6.3).

Reporting can be within and between the teams and is usually infrequent. Reporting is typically one way and does not include an intense

Table 6.3 **Instances of communication**

Team communication
Debating differences of
• Personal opinions
• Professional vantage points
• Artistic and creative issues
Clarifications of technical issues
Request for information
Clarifying personal issues
Group meetings
Exchange of information

cycle of debate and clarification. Within the context of team charter, reporting is part of professional performance, whereas communication is part of behavioral issues. As a consequence, communication takes place often.

One of the distinguishing characteristics of communication is that it is charged with and often tempered by feelings, perceptions, and emotions. Personal communication is usually voice-to-voice or face-to-face. Besides, personal and enterprise communication of information transfer often takes place through intonation and body language. Additionally, sometimes, team members might communicate occasionally and casually on the subjects of cost, schedule, and scope.

Needless to say, communication will have a greater impact on the ultimate success of the project. Therefore, in addition to providing guidelines for factual reporting, organizations should provide ample tools and procedures to allow people to enhance personal communication. In project-friendly organizations, the team members freely share their progress, opinions, and concerns with each other. This free exchange of information will in turn result in a cooperative spirit and synergistic innovation among team members.

The lines of communication are usually used both ways during the project execution. Unidirectional communication between individuals suggests that team performance is poor when such communication is limited to the impersonal task of the distribution of progress reports and selected data.

In productive and high-performing teams, communication occurs very frequently within the team, occasionally with people who are outside the team and within the performing organization, and much less frequently with people who are within the client organization. Healthy communication leads to cooperation, and—along with frequent communication—are the two major attributes of productive and cohesive teams. If there was no communication, it is almost certain that conflicts would develop, leading to extensive negotiations and conflict resolutions.

Conflict Management and Negotiations

Each project team member comes with a different experience, knowledge, intellect level, and personality type. Additionally, conflict occurs due to incompatible goals, thoughts, or emotions between individuals in the team. Obviously, any team or a group of highly skilled and exceptionally creative individuals will interpret facts and events differently. If the intellectual diversity is communicated and debated properly, the most appropriate solution can be identified easily and amicably. However, it may not always happen.

Most people have a general instinctive tendency to avoid all conflict and prefer harmony. Open and free communication will forestall the vast majority of disagreements and conflicts within the team. On the other hand, intellectual diversity generates creative solutions and innovation. Intellectual diversity is a mild form of conflict, and it usually results in innovative deliverables; and, therefore, it leads to increased team cohesiveness. It is crucial for the organization to foster an environment that promotes open and constructive discussion among team members. An enlightened and constructive approach is to view minor differences as a potentially positive component of the project team experience, and as a catalyst for innovation and creativity. This is particularly true if it is always controlled and not allowed to become a serious disagreement.

If minor differences in viewpoint are identified early and resolved properly, conflicts can be avoided. One must remember that poor communication will cause or exacerbate conflicts while negotiations and compromises will remedy or minimize major conflicts. If the intellectual diversity, with respect to people or task-related issues, is allowed to emerge as a serious disagreement and possibly evolve into major conflicts, project performance will suffer. In such cases, the project manager will be left with no option but to employ formal conflict-management techniques and intense negotiations.

Personal conflicts are somewhat common in traditional projects and virtual project teams that are formed without an effective supporting structure. These conflicts are hardly ever discovered before the occurrence of major project shortfalls (Table 6.4).

Notably, personal conflicts will manifest themselves as technical disagreements, or worse yet, as major technical conflicts. In turn, these technical conflicts will cause shortfalls in the schedule, budget, resource allocation, and legal concerns.

Conflict resolution will not remove the poor project performance up to the point of the discovery of the conflict; but rather it might minimize the future damage to the project progress. A sophisticated enterprise should have tools and procedures to resolve serious disagreements and major conflicts. Communication and team civility are somewhat akin to fire-prevention techniques while conflict management and negotiations can be regarded analogous to the fire-fighting techniques.

Table 6.4 Sources of conflict

People issues	<ul><li>Differences in personality attributes</li><li>Diverse background (family, ethnic, and culture)</li><li>Attitude toward sharing of information</li><li>Level of commitment</li><li>Differences in team spirit among members</li><li>Civility</li><li>Promptness</li></ul>
Technical issues	<ul><li>Sharing resources</li><li>Cost constraints</li><li>Time constraints</li><li>Schedule constraints</li><li>Risk perceptions and attitude toward risk</li><li>Ambiguity associated with scope</li><li>Quality standards and requirement</li></ul>

Project Team Performance Model

Through defining processes and roles, project teams can establish both predictability and openness with all the team activities. This environment will foster clarity and transparency in communication, which will in turn set the stage for a successful project (Figure 6.1).

Predictability, openness, and transparency are important factors in establishing trust among the project team members. Moreover, it is important to address personal and professional aspirations of team members by presenting opportunities to build competencies through mentoring, training, knowledge sharing, learning, and education. Addressing individual needs for growth promotes mutual trust and respect. Trust encourages project team members to collaborate, network, and innovate. By establishing trust, leaders can manage changes, mitigate conflicts—a deterrent to project performance—and transform project stakeholders into a cohesive project team. Given that establishing trust usually takes time and that projects are time bound, the task of building trust among team members becomes even more challenging. This model (Figure 6.1) facilitates the leadership behavior necessary to develop effective teams and to create synergy among the team members.

Productive Teams and Knowledge Management

Professional growth is a direct outcome of the learning that happens when teams work together harmoniously. Therefore, at the level of the individual team member, measures of team success could be professional growth

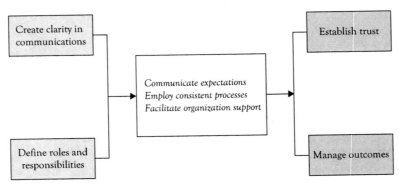

Figure 6.1 Team performance

as a result of knowledge gained by working with other team members collaboratively. The characteristics of productive and harmonious teams are low turnover and focus on individuals and tasks and work overall.

It is widely recognized that knowledge is a key economic resource. Specifically, knowledge sharing and the resultant new knowledge creation and innovation are critical for organizations to become and remain competitive. Projects in general and global projects in particular provide opportunities to learn from each other and enhance knowledge sharing.

Learning from each other to enhance the capabilities of the enterprise and at individual levels is desired for potential growth opportunities. However, knowledge sharing in international collaborations and global projects is not without pitfalls. From an enterprise standpoint, organizational knowledge that is proprietary—a critical resource for creating and sustaining competitive advantage as competitors cannot easily replicate it—will no longer be confined within the organization. From an individual standpoint, businesses would not like to share proprietary knowledge unless the rewards outweigh the perceived value of the knowledge. Thus, it becomes a challenge to retain the competitive edge of organizations while participating in global projects. Organizations will have to make the distinction between the core competitive knowledge that needs to be retained and other relevant knowledge that is necessary to share for effective collaboration and successful completion of global projects. The project manager and project teams must recognize this distinction in sharing knowledge.

Research has shown that social capital is comprised of shared vision, trust, and social ties in an organization. Social capital plays an important role in knowledge sharing and knowledge transfer. Both are essential to promote synergy and team performance. However, trust cannot be built in a team if knowledge levels among its members are high, which is common when team members are diverse. On the other hand, the knowledge of the team members tends to improve communication, and the diversity of knowledge is likely to enhance creativity in problem solving. Needless to say, communication is critical for knowledge sharing, problem solving, and decision making in project teams. With the increase in team social capital, knowledge sharing becomes more effective and helps teams to be more productive.

Effective Use of Technology for Project Teams

Technology assumes importance in the context of project management due to the greater challenges in today's technology-enabled work environment. Nowadays, technology tools are routinely used for collaboration, communication, and the deployment of project management practices. It is becoming common practice for even colocated project teams to use electronic medium for these purposes. Technology can play a major role in supporting project managers in leading projects effectively and efficiently.

In addition to capturing and storing information with easy access, technology can be used for developing and deploying project management processes and performance monitoring systems. Several project management software tools are available to manage project management tasks such as developing detailed schedules, estimating cost, allocating resources, assessing and managing risk, monitoring progress, and measuring project performance. Technology can efficiently and effectively help the project team accomplish the following project management functions:

- Document the defined project roles and implement related processes.
- Establish formal and consistent processes.
- Communicate expectations of processes and roles.
- Communicate openly among all the project team members, including virtual teams.
- Monitor and manage project outcomes.

Specifically, technology plays a major role in helping the project manager to develop and formalize project processes and establish channels of open communication. With the appropriate use of technological tools, the project team can access organizational and tacit knowledge of past projects and historical data. This information can help project teams improve their project performance. For effective capturing of lessons learned, project managers must perform project reviews throughout the project management life cycle. Project managers should review project performance periodically during the project execution phase, and document important lessons learned when ideas and experiences are fresh in the minds of the project team members. This approach will help project managers capture both tacit and explicit knowledge that their project team members possess.

Project managers can achieve a higher level of continuous improvement in project performance by applying numerous technology tools throughout the project management life cycle:

- Selecting projects by using knowledge-based decision systems consisting of quantitative and qualitative criteria
- Developing a resource breakdown structure for the project environment and keeping it current by using resource cost information from historical project data and resource database systems
- Developing project plans and scope with the help of historical data from knowledge repositories related to project plans and scope definitions.
- Estimating—accurately and realistically—project costs by using historical cost and effort estimation and earned value data of past projects.
- Developing a WBS by using standardized WBS packages maintained in database systems
- Developing a project schedule by using historical schedule data and "After Action Review" information from knowledge repositories
- Managing resources by using actual resource usage data from similar projects
- Reducing risk

In essence, technology can help project managers improve the project processes that are used in order to manage project complexity, project integration, and resource utilization.

Going beyond these processes, technology can help project managers in managing teams effectively by promoting open communication, learning, knowledge transfer, and productivity. Project managers may also choose to develop electronic yellow pages that list project experts in specific interest groups, such as scope definition, scheduling, cost estimating, and risk management. Other technologies such as video conferences, the Internet, and an Intranet can help project managers lead projects using virtual project teams. These technologies help project managers communicate effectively with their virtual project teams and integrate project tasks effectively.

Technologies provide project management tools for planning and web-based support systems, which are essential for communication, conflict resolution, knowledge sharing, and integration of complex projects. The shift to sophisticated project management tools, driven by factors such as project complexities and diverse cultures requiring new management skills, is having a profound impact on project leadership. These results assume importance in the present context because methods of communication, decision making, soliciting commitment, and risk sharing shift the management style to a team-centered and self-directed form of project control.

Desirable Attributes of High-Performance Project Teams

By developing a team charter and adhering to it, a desirable outcome is facilitated that offers an environment of harmony, trust, teamwork, respect, dedication, and commitment among the project team members. Most of the characteristics of this work environment cannot be prescribed and such a team environment is the true indication of a productive and high-performing team. These attitudinal attributes are the subtle symptoms of a high-performing team, albeit possibly prompted and assisted by the procedures and guidelines prescribing the professional performance and personal interaction of the team members. Project success, project team success, and indicators of high performance are the desirable contributions of project team members and reflect a positive attitude of the team members.

The presence of the desirable attitudes and attributes of team members can be inferred, through the success of behavioral attributes. These behavioral attributes, such as communication, intellectual diversity, and conflict management, are relatively easy to measure. To carry that one step further, positive attitudinal attributes can also be inferred from the repeated successes of the project team in delivering project success and project team success. Unfortunately, direct testing and measurement of these attributes are difficult. The presence of positive attitudinal attributes can only be inferred based on the quality of the behavioral patterns.

A casual characterization of the presence of desirable attitudinal attributes, such as dedication to a project goal, would be to determine if, and to what extent, an individual team member is concerned with the success of the project team as a whole. The level of team spirit would be reflected by the team member's response to a hypothetical situation: *What would one of the team members do if he or she noticed a flaw in the project deliverable, a flaw that did not impact his or her individual deliverable, but a flaw that he or she could remedy quickly and easily?*

Pure virtual teams are probably relatively rare, although pure traditional teams still exist in some project environments. It is always helpful to know where a project environment maps on the continuum between extreme virtual and extreme traditional in as much as the differences between the traditional and virtual teams must always be on the forefront of the considerations for the virtual team. The commonality between virtual and traditional teams should always be defined and enhanced. Furthermore, providing detailed and appropriate formalized procedures will ultimately result in bona fide team spirit and teamwork in both team structures (Table 6.5).

Table 6.5 *Traditional versus virtual teams*

Traditional teams	<ul><li>Assistance of body language in communications</li><li>Assistance of personal charm in relationships</li><li>The effectiveness of charismatic project managers</li><li>Ease of personal debates and clarifications</li></ul>
Virtual teams	<ul><li>Reliance on written communications</li><li>Reliance on<ul><li>Formal planning</li><li>Formal change management</li><li>Individual competencies</li></ul></li><li>Careful matching of<ul><li>Team members to team</li><li>Team members to their duties</li></ul></li></ul>

Communication and information sharing through regular face-to-face communication are norms for traditional teams. By comparison, conceivably all of the interaction among virtual team members is conducted through means that are sometimes characterized as impersonal using media such as text-to-text, sometimes voice-to-voice, and rarely face-to-face methods. The bulk of the communication is done asynchronously using e-mails and other electronic media. However, occasionally, traditional projects use virtual team tools such as e-mails, portals, and teleconferencing to free up the team members from traveling to remote sites for project work. Furthermore, team members who live in reasonable proximity of one another form a virtual team for the purposes of convenience and operation efficiency.

Virtual teams rely only on written text for most of their communication. Therefore, to minimize misunderstanding, and more importantly to be mindful of personal feelings, there will have to be extensive formality in the conduct of most communication and reporting functions of virtual teams. Full development of positive attitudinal attributes will take longer to develop in virtual teams than it does in traditional teams.

Many of the people skills that work well with traditional teams do not work as well with virtual teams. Sometimes they do not work at all. The reason is simply that the bulk of the communication of the traditional teams takes place in a nonverbal form. Although, to some extent, one can capture the mood or feelings of a sender of the message using clues such as the choice of words or the tone of the language in written messages of virtual teams, it is difficult to establish effective communication quickly in the virtual environment. Therefore, traditional team-related processes might have to be modified for use with virtual teams. When developing, or adapting, processes for virtual teams, one would need to address how and when the traditional team procedures are suitable for virtual teams. Sometimes, new guidelines might have to be created for those issues that are specific to virtual teams.

The virtual team members must be continually aware and sensitive to the scarcity of the conventional human interaction in virtual teams. In virtual teams, there is no opportunity for a continuous stream of questions and answers as there is in traditional teams. Consequently, there is an extraordinary pressure, at least compared to the traditional teams, to be accurate, succinct, clear, and direct, when information is transmitted to other team members.

The mode of communication and tools of communication of the virtual team are commonly identified as the root causes of the success or failure of virtual teams. However, one of the frequent reasons for the failure of some of the virtual teams is not necessarily a shortfall in information flow or in technical competency and physical performance issues, but rather the fact the virtual teams are denied the bulk of the traditional modes of person-to-person communication. As it is for traditional teams, a comprehensive set of processes and guidelines for behavioral attributes and professional performance is the critical first step for virtual team norms.

Team Maturity

Project teams are composed of individuals and each member comes with a unique personality, and the motivation to join the team is different for different individuals. Each team member's behavior and interactions toward the team can lead to positive or negative actions. The maturity level of the team would largely depend on bringing individuals together and aligning their actions to the team purpose by establishing team norms, processes, roles, and responsibilities (Table 6.6).

Organizations may choose to adapt the five levels of maturity shown in Table 6.6 or modify it to suit their specific needs. In general, the maturity level ranges from the lowest level of little teamwork and the presence of very few processes (level 0) to the presence of highest levels of cooperation, collaboration, trust, synergy, and innovation (level 4). The transition from level 0 to level 4 demands conscious effort and recognition of the importance of team development.

Team Performance Measurement System

The purpose of any team performance measurement system is to improve its productivity and effectiveness. The measurement system should not be such that team members attempt to optimize for metrics of performance thereby sacrificing quality. Therefore, performance measures should help

Table 6.6 Maturity levels of project teams

Level 0	Level 1	Level 2	Level 3	Level 4
Unfamiliarity	Relations with	Identity with	Team focus	Self-managed
Lack of role	team	team	Role maturity	team
clarity	Roles defined	Role	Process	Mutual support
No team	Communica-	performance	maturity	of roles
procedures	tion process	Established	Team cohesion	Established
Individual focus	Mutual	processes	Mutual	processes
Existence of	influence	Mutual respect	responsibility	Team cohesion
conflicts	Conflicts	Shared	Importance to	Collaboration
Social loafing	addressed	responsibility	team	Cooperation
Leader-	Social loafing	Importance to	Team charter	Synergy
acknowledged	addressed	team	defined	Standard team
Self-identity	Leader	Team charter	Trust among	charter
	accepted	defined	the team	Knowledge
	Social identity	Trust among	Risk	management
		the team	management	**Emotional**
		Risk	**Group mood**	**intelligence**
		management		
		Group emotion		

Source: Adapted from Adams and Anantatmula (2010).

the team and not necessarily just senior management. Furthermore, an empowered team must design its performance measurement system around a handful of measures and track and monitor progress against these measures.[5]

Questions:

1. Define and develop metrics of team performance.
2. Explain how management's values impact the performance of the business.
3. Share an example of when you experienced both micromanagement and delegation.
4. Differentiate among project, proposal, and portfolio teams.
5. Describe the importance of a team charter.
6. What are the benefits of using a team charter?

---

[5] Meyer (2014).

CHAPTER 7

Sustaining Effectiveness of Project Teams

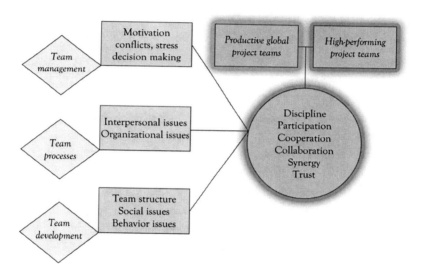

Preview

This chapter presents a summary of what is presented and discussed in the book along with a few guidelines for assessing and sustaining effectiveness and success of project teams.

Projects are vehicles for organizations to meet their strategic objectives and operational goals. They are executed in teams and, as such, being a member of a team is an inevitable feature of modern work life. A project team comprises *a selected group of individuals with complimentary skills and disciplines who are required to work together on interdependent and interrelated tasks for a predetermined period to meet a specific purpose or goal.* Project teams can be traditional colocated teams, virtual teams, and global project teams. A few common attributes of a project team are: common purpose or goal, interdependence due to mutual accountability and collective responsibility, diverse skills, information sharing, and collaborative efforts.

In general, projects are managed using teams in a work environment that is complex for two reasons: first, each project is unique, and second, conditions for team selection and motivation are often far from ideal. In addition to uniqueness and complexity, unfamiliarity is often described as one of the characteristics of projects and, as a result, projects are often associated with change. Consequently, successful project performance requires strong leadership, which provides vision and ability to cope with change.

In effective project teams, each team member assigns preference to team's objectives over individual differences and personal goals. Project managers should make an effort to align individual aspirations, and personal and professional goals with the project goals. One must be sensitive to the needs, aspirations, and goals of all other team members; it will influence the team's performance and success. Even though each member of the team is a distinct individual with strong opinions about a lot of things, the team needs to have a single and identifiable direction for its activities. Effective teams create synergy among the team members to enhance creativity, productivity, and decision making. Team effectiveness will also have an impact on satisfaction of the individual team members and on the quality of their team assignment deliverable.

This book is aimed to provide an overview of selecting, structuring, developing, and managing project teams to improve collaborative effort and productivity in managing projects successfully, underlining the importance of various aspects of structuring and developing project teams:

- A team structure design largely depends on the organization structure and culture to promote teamwork.
- Organizations must focus on developing and sustaining team-related processes that would ensure continuity and continual improvement in team development.

- Project teams require both management and leadership as stress and conflicts are bound to occur. Furthermore, it is a challenge to manage and guide team members to work collaboratively while dividing the work and multiplying the success. The key is to align goals or aspirations of individual team members with the project goals, and invest time in understanding individual strengths and building competencies wherever necessary.
- Obstacles of political, cultural, virtual, and regional differences of global project teams influence the structure of global teams and it differs from that of a traditional project team. Communication, culture, and leadership assume importance in managing global projects. A formal approach to team development and management processes is necessary. Knowledge management and communication are key aspects of global project teams.
- Developing a project team charter helps project teams to perform cohesively and manage project outcomes effectively. The team charter should clearly specify the goals and structure of the team, desirable performance attributes, performance guidelines and metrics, and behavioral expectations.

One cannot forget the rising number of Generation Y professionals (born in 1980 and after) who are part of the workforce and their impact on project teams. They would expect and believe in less emphasis on hierarchy and greater responsibility. Monetary benefit is less motivating than working relations and meaningful work.

Effectiveness of Project Teams

Organizations should focus on establishing organizational factors and team factors that would promote project team effectiveness and efficiency while keeping project success factors in mind.

The presence of organizational and team factors outlined in Table 7.1 defines the level of maturity in developing project teams. Organizations

Table 7.1 Project team effectiveness

Project success factors	Organizational factors	Project team factors
• Completing within cost • Completing within time • Meeting project scope • Meeting quality • Meeting customer needs • Achieving satisfaction of key stakeholders • Achieving financial success • Achieving commercial success	• Formalized project management practices • Team-selection processes • Team-development processes • Competency building • Collaborative culture • Conflict management • Top management support • Portfolio management • Project management office (PMO)	*Define* • Role definition and clarity • Empowerment • Delegation • Accountability • Team charter • Communication process *Expect* • Cooperation • Collaboration • Synergy • Trust among team members • Emotional intelligence • Conflict resolution • Innovation

may choose to develop five levels of maturity, ranging from little team-work and the presence of very few processes (level 0) to the presence of highest levels of cooperation, collaboration, trust, synergy, and innovation (level 4). However, these maturity levels are organization specific and would depend on the number of projects, project size, number of employers engaged in projects, and so on. Irrespective of the maturity model that an organization may develop to assess team processes and team effectiveness, it is important to review them periodically to explore options for continuous improvement of performance and effectiveness of project teams.

Bibliography

Adams, S., and V. Anantatmula. 2010. "Social and Behavioral Influences on Project Team Process." *Project Management Journal* 41, no. 4, pp. 89–98.

Adenfelt, M., and K. Lagerström. 2006. "Enabling Knowledge Creation and Sharing in Transnational Projects." *International Journal of Project Management* 24, no. 3, pp. 191–98.

Anantatmula, V. 2005. "Outcomes of Knowledge Management Initiatives." *International Journal of Knowledge Management* 1, no. 2, pp. 50–67.

Anantatmula, V. 2008. "Role of Technology in Project Manager Performance Model." *Project Management Journal* 39, no. 1, pp. 34–48.

Anantatmula, V. 2010. "Impact of Cultural Differences on Knowledge Management in Global Projects." *The VINE: Journal of Information and Knowledge Management Systems* 40, no. 3, pp. 239–53.

Anantatmula, V. 2010. "Project Manager Leadership Role in Improving Project Performance." *Engineering Management Journal* 22, no. 1, pp. 13–22.

Anantatmula, V., and B. Shrivastav. 2012. "Evolution of Project Teams for Generation Y Workforce." *International Journal of Managing Projects in Business* 5, no. 1, pp. 9–25.

Anantatmula, V., and M. Thomas. 2010. "Managing Global Projects: A Structured Approach for Better Performance." *Project Management Journal* 41, no. 2, pp. 60–72.

Ariely, D. 2008. *Predictably Irrational*. New York: HarperCollins.

Austin, R. 1996. *Measuring and Managing Performance in Organizations*. New York: Dorset House.

Awakul, P., and S. Ogunlana. 2002. "The Effect of Attitudinal Differences on Interface Conflicts in Large Scale Construction Projects: A Case Study." *Construction Management and Economics* 20, no. 4, pp. 365–77.

Barua, A., C.-H. S. Lee, and A.B. Whinston. 1995. "Incentives and Computing Systems for Team-Based Organizations." *Organization Science* 6, no. 4, pp. 487–504.

Belbin, R.M. 2003. *Team Roles at Work*. Oxford: Butterworth-Heinemann.

Bosch-Sijtsema, P.M., V. Ruohomäki, and M. Vartiainen. 2009. "Knowledge Work Productivity in Distributed Teams." *Journal of Knowledge Management* 13, no. 6, pp. 533–46.

Bowers, C.A., C.C. Braun, and B.B. Morgan Jr. 1997. "Team Workload: Its Meaning and Measurement." In *Team Performance and Measurement: Theory, Methods, and Applications*, 85–108. Mahwah, NJ: Lawrence Erlbaum Associates.

Brahm, T., and F. Kunze. 2012. "The Role of Trust Climate in Virtual Teams." *Journal of Managerial Psychology* 27, no. 6, pp. 595–614.

Brass, D., J. Galaskiewicz, H. Greve, and W. Tsai. 2004. "Taking Stock of Networks and Organizations: A Multilevel Perspective." *Academy of Management Journal* 47, no. 6, pp. 795–817.

Carter, D.R., P.W. Seely, J. Dogosta, L.A. DeChurch, and S.J Zaccaro. 2015. "Leadership for Global Virtual Teams: Facilitating Teamwork Processes." In *Leading Global Teams*, 225–52. New York: Springer.

Cohen, S.G., and D.E. Bailey. 1997. "What Makes Teams Work: Group Effectiveness Research from the Shop Floor to the Executive Suite." *Journal of Management* 23, no. 3, pp. 239–90.

Creasy, T., and V.S. Anantatmula. 2013. "From Every Direction-How Personality Traits and Dimensions of Project Managers Can Conceptually Affect Project Success." *Project Management Journal* 44, no. 6, pp. 36–51.

Damian, D.E., and D. Zowghi. 2003. "An Insight into the Interplay between Culture, Conflict and Distance in Globally Distributed Requirements Negotiations." In *Proceedings of the 36th Annual Hawaii International Conference on System Sciences*.

Dinsmore, P.C. 1984. *Human Factors in Project Management*. Rev. ed. New York: American Management Association.

Druskat, V., and S. Wolff. 2001. "Building the Emotional Intelligence of Groups." *Harvard Business Review* 79, no. 3, pp. 80–91.

Dubé, L., and G. Paré. 2001. "Global Virtual Teams." *Communications of the ACM* 44, no. 12, pp. 71–73.

Dyer, W.G. 1995. *Team Building: Current Issues and New Alternatives*. 3rd ed. Reading, MA: Addison-Wesley.

Edmondson, A., R. Bohmer, and G. Pisano. 2001. "Speeding Up Team Learning." *Harvard Business Review* 79, no. 9, pp. 125–34.

Eunson, B. 2014. *Communicating in the 21st Century*. 3rd ed. Milton, Qld: John Wiley and Sons Australia.

Ferraro, G.P., and E.K. Briody. 2013. *The Cultural Dimension of Global Business*. 7th ed. Boston: Pearson.

Feser, C., F. Mayol, and R. Srinivasan. 2015. "Decoding Leadership: What Really Matters." *McKinsey Quarterly*. www.mckinsey.com/insights/leading_in_the_21st_century/decoding_leadership_what_really_matters

Fiedler, F.E. 1996. "Research on Leadership Selection and Training: One View of the Future." *Administrative Science Quarterly*, pp. 241–50.

Fiore, S.M. 2008. "Interdisciplinarity as Teamwork: How the Science of Teams Can Inform Team Science." *Small Group Research* 39, no. 3, pp. 251–77.

Fisher, R., W. Ury, and B. Patton. 2011. *Getting to Yes: Negotiating Agreement Without Giving in*. New York: Penguin.

Furumo, K. 2009. "The Impact of Conflict and Conflict Management Style on Deadbeats and Deserters in Virtual Teams." *Journal of Computer Information Systems* 49, no. 4, pp. 66–73.

Gabrenya, W.K., and P.B. Smith. 2015. "Project GLOBE for Scientists and Practitioners: Drawing Clarity from Controversy." In *Leading Global Teams*, 33–65. New York: Springer.

Gardiner, P.D., and J.E.L. Simmons. 1998. "Conflict in Small- and Medium-Sized Projects: Case of Partnering to the Rescue." *Journal of Management in Engineering* 14, no. 1, pp. 35–40.

Garvin, D.A., and M.A. Roberto. 2001. "What You Don't Know About Making Decisions." *Harvard Business Review* 79, no. 8, pp. 108–16.

Garvin, D.A., and M.A. Roberto. 2003. "What You Don't Know About Making Decisions." *IEEE Engineering Management Review* 31, no. 2, pp. 3–10.

Gehring, D.R. 2007. "Applying Traits of Leadership to Project Management." *Project Management Journal* 38, no. 1, pp. 44–54.

Gibson, C.B., and S.G. Cohen. 2003. *Virtual Teams that Work Creating Conditions for Virtual Team Effectiveness*. San Francisco: Jossey-Bass.

Goris, J.R. 2007. "Effects of Satisfaction with Communication on the Relationship between Individual-Job Congruence and Job Performance/Satisfaction." *Journal of Management Development* 26, no. 8, pp. 737–52.

Hagen, M., and S. Park. 2013. "Ambiguity Acceptance as a Function of Project Management: A New Critical Success Factor." *Project Management Journal* 44, no. 2, pp. 52–66.

Hall, E.T. 1984. *The Dance of Life: The Other Dimension of Time*. 2nd ed. Garden City, NY: Anchor Press/Doubleday.

Hashim, N., and N. Chileshe. 2011. "Exploration of Project Managers Competencies for Managing Multiple Project Environments (MMPE) within Australian Organizations." *Lecture, 8th Project Management Australia Conference*, January 1.

Hersey, P., and K. Blanchard. 1996. "Great Ideas Revisited: Revisiting the Life-cycle Theory of Leadership." *Training & Development* 50, no. 1, pp. 43–47.

Hinds, P.J., and D.E. Bailey. 2003. "Out of Sight, Out of Sync: Understanding Conflict in Distributed Teams." *Organization Science* 14, no. 6, pp. 615–32.

Hoegl, M., and H.G. Gemuenden. 2001. "Teamwork Quality and the Success of Innovative Projects." *Organization Science* 12, no. 4, pp. 435–49.

Hofstede, G.H. 1997. *Cultures and Organizations: Software of the Mind*. London: McGraw-Hill.

Hofstede, G.H. 1980. *Culture's Consequences: International Differences in Work-Related Values*. Beverly Hills, CA: Sage Publications.

Hofstede, G.H., G.J. Hofstede, and M. Minkov. 2010. *Cultures and Organizations: Software of the Mind: Intercultural Cooperation and Its Importance for Survival*. Revised and Expanded 3rd ed. New York: McGraw-Hill.

Hogg, M.A. 2006. "Social Identity Theory." In *Contemporary Social Psychological Theories*, 111–36.

Holt, S., and V. Green. 2009. "Leadership and Culture: Examining the Relationship Between Cultural Background and Leadership Perceptions." *Journal of Global Business Issues* 3, no. 2, pp. 149–64.

Hyväri, I. 2006. "Project Management Effectiveness in Project-Oriented Business Organizations." *International Journal of Project Management* 24, no. 3, pp. 216–25.

Jaeger, A.M., and R.N. Kanungo. 1990. *Management in Developing Countries*. New York: Routledge.

Janis, I.L. 1982. *Groupthink: Psychological Studies of Policy Decisions and Fiascoes*. 2nd ed. Boston: Houghton Mifflin.

Jarvenpaa, S.L., and D.E. Leidner. 1999. "Communication and Trust in Global Virtual Teams." *Organization Science* 10, no. 6, pp. 791–815.

Jehn, K.A. 1995. "A Multimethod Examination of the Benefits and Detriments of Intragroup Conflict." *Administrative Science Quarterly* 40, no. 2, pp. 256–82.

Jones, R.G., and W. Lindley. 1998. "Issues in the Transition to Teams." *Journal of Business and Psychology* 13, no. 1, pp. 31–40.

Katzenbach, J., and D. Smith. 1993. "The Discipline of Teams." *Harvard Business Review*, pp. 111–20.

Kerzner, H. 2009. *Project Management: A Systems Approach to Planning, Scheduling, and Controlling*. 10th ed. New York: Wiley.

Kezsbom, D. 1995. "Team Work: The Magic of Interaction." In *Proceedings of the 1995 Annual Seminar Symposium–Project Management Institute*, pp. 477–81.

Khan, M.S. 2012. "Role of Trust and Relationships in Geographically Distributed Teams: Exploratory Study on Development Sector." *International Journal of Networking and Virtual Organizations* 10, no. 1, pp. 40–58.

Khan, M.S., R.J. Breitenecker, and E.J. Schwarz. 2014. "Entrepreneurial Team Locus of Control: Diversity and Trust." *Management Decision* 52, no. 6, pp. 1057–81.

Kirkman, B.L., and J.E. Mathieu. 2005. "The Dimensions and Antecedents of Team Virtuality." *Journal of Management* 31, no. 5, pp. 700–18.

Kirkman, B.L., R.G. Jones, and D.L. Shapiro. 2000. "Why Do Employees Resist Teams? Examining the 'Resistance Barrier' to Work Team Effectiveness." *International Journal of Conflict Management* 11, no. 1, pp. 74–92.

Knapp, M.T., R.J. Breitenecker, and M.S. Khan. 2015. "Achievement Motivation Diversity and Entrepreneurial Team Performance: The Mediating Role of Cohesion." *European Journal of International Management* 9, no. 5, pp. 593–613.

Kupperschmidt, B.R. 2000. "Multigeneration Employees: Strategies for Effective Management." *The Health Care Manager* 19, no. 1, pp. 65–76.

Kuprenas, J.A. 2003. "Implementation and Performance of a Matrix Organization Structure." *International Journal of Project Management* 21, no. 1, pp. 51–62.

Lacerenza, C.N., S. Zajac, N. Savage, and E. Salas. 2015. "Team Training for Global Virtual Teams: Strategies for Success." In *Leading Global Teams: Translating Multidisciplinary Science to Practice*, 91–121. New York: Springer.

Laslo, Z., and A.I. Goldberg. 2008. "Resource Allocation under Uncertainty in a Multi-Project Matrix Environment: Is Organizational Conflict Inevitable?" *International Journal of Project Management* 26, no. 8, pp. 773–88.

Lencioni, P. 2002. *The Five Dysfunctions of a Team: A Leadership Fable.* Manga ed. San Fransisco, CA: Jossey-Bass.

MacCormack, A., T. Forbath, P. Brooks, and P. Kalaher. 2007. "From Outsourcing to Global Collaboration: New Ways to Build Competitiveness." *Harvard Business Review.*

Marks, M.A., J.E. Mathieu, and S.J. Zaccaro. 2001. "A Temporally Based Framework and Taxonomy of Team Process." *Academy of Management Review* 26, no. 3, pp. 356–76.

Marmer, C. 1998. "Building Teams Across Borders." *Global Workforce*, November, pp. 13–17.

Mayer, J.D., and P. Salovey. 1997. "What Is Emotional Intelligence?" In *Emotional Development and Emotional Intelligence: Implications for Educators*, 3–31. New York: Basic Books.

Meyer, E. 2014. *The Culture Map: Breaking Through the Invisible Barriers of Global Business.* Philadelphia, PA: Perseus Books.

Miloslavic, S.A., J.L. Wildman, and A.L. Thayer. 2015. "Structuring Successful Global Virtual Teams." In *Leading Global Teams: Translating Multidisciplinary Science to Practice*, 67–87. New York: Springer.

Mintzberg, H. 1979. *The Structure of Organizations.* Englewood Cliffs, NJ: Prentice Hall.

Mohammed, S., L. Ferzandi, and K. Hamilton. 2010. "Metaphor No More: A 15-Year Review of the Team Mental Model Construct." *Journal of Management* 36, no. 4, pp. 876–910.

Montoya-Weiss, M.M., A.P. Massey, and M. Song. 2001. "Getting It Together: Temporal Coordination and Conflict Management in Global Virtual Teams." *Academy of Management Journal* 44, no. 6, pp. 1251–262.

Moore, C. n.d. *Negotiation.*

Muriithi, N., and L. Crawford. 2003. "Approaches to Project Management in Africa: Implications for International Development Projects." *International Journal of Project Management* 21, no. 5, pp. 309–19.

Nisen, M. 2013. "Moneyball at Work: They've Discovered What Really Makes a Good Employee." Retrieved July 11, 2015 from www.businessinsider.com/big-data-in-the-workplace-2013-5

Olson, G.M., and J.S. Olson. 2000. "Distance Matters." *Human-Computer Interaction* 15, no. 2, pp. 139–79.

Palumbo, C. 2014. "A Model of Organizational Cultures Predictive of Well-Being: From the Organization of Work to Broader Social." *Universal Journal of Psychology* 2, no. 7, pp. 213–17.

Patnayakuni, R., A. Rai, and A. Tiwana. 2007. "Systems Development Process Improvement: A Knowledge Integration Perspective." *IEEE Transactions on Engineering Management* 54, no. 2, pp. 286–300.

Paul, S., P. Seetharaman, I. Samarah, and P.P. Mykytyn. 2004. "Impact of Heterogeneity and Collaborative Conflict Management Style on the Performance of Synchronous Global Virtual Teams." *Information & Management* 41, no. 3, pp. 303–21.

Pinto, M., and J. Pinto. 1990. "Project Team Communication and Cross-functional Cooperation in New Program Development." *Journal of Product Innovation Management* 7, no. 3, pp. 200–12.

Project Helping RSS. "Volunteering Benefits—Project Helping." https://projecthelping.org/volunteering-benefits/ (accessed November 7, 2015).

Rad, P., and V. Anantatmula. 2010. *Successful Project Management Practices*. Bingley: Emerald Group Publishing.

Robbins, S.P. 1979a. *Managing Organizational Conflict: A Nontraditional Approach*. Englewood Cliffs, NJ: Prentice Hall.

Robbins, S.P. 1979b. *Organizational Behavior*. Englewood Cliffs, NJ: Prentice Hall.

Robbins, S.P., and R. Stuart-Kotze. 1986. *Management: Concepts and Practices*. Canadian Edition ed. Toronto, Ontario: Prentice Hall Canada.

Rottier, B., N. Ripmeester, and A. Bush. 2011. "Separated by a Common Translation? How the British and the Dutch Communicate." *Pediatric Pulmonology* 46, no. 4, pp. 409–11.

Sarker, S., and S. Sahay. 2002. "Implications of Space and Time for Distributed Work: An Interpretive Study of US–Norwegian Systems Development Teams." *IEEE Computer Society*.

Schein, E. 1993. *Organizational Culture and Leadership*. In *Classics of Organization Theory*. Fort Worth, TX: Harcourt College Publishers.

Schweiger, D.M. 1998. "Networking Global Style." *Business Economic Review*, January–March, pp. 3–6.

Scott, C.P.R., and J.L. Wildman. 2015. "Culture, Communication, and Conflict: A Review of the Global Virtual Team Literature." In *Leading Global Teams*, 13–32. New York: Springer.

Seltzer, J., and B. Bass. 1990. "Transformational Leadership: Beyond Initiation and Consideration." *Journal of Management* 16, no. 4, pp. 693–703.

Seta, C.E., P.B. Paulus, and R.A. Baron. 2000. *Effective Human Relations: A Guide to People at Work.* 4th ed. Boston: Allyn and Bacon.

Shuster, H.D. 1999. *Teaming for Quality the Right Way for the Right Reasons.* Newton Square, PA: Project Management Institute.

Simon, B., and T.F. Pettigrew. 1990. "Social Identity and Perceived Group Homogeneity: Evidence for the Ingroup Homogeneity Effect." *European Journal of Social Psychology* 20, no. 4, pp. 269–86.

"Six Teams that Changed the World." 2006. Secrets of Greatness: Great Teams. *Fortune Magazine,* May 31. http://archive.fortune.com/2006/05/31/magazines/fortune/sixteams_greatteams_fortune_061206/index.htm (accessed November 10, 2015).

Smith, P.B., and J. Noakes. 1996. "A Process Stage Model of Cross-cultural Teams." In *Handbook of Work Group Psychology.* John Wiley & Sons.

Stahl, G.K., K. Mäkelä, L. Zander, and M.L. Maznevski. 2010. "A Look at the Bright Side of Multicultural Team Diversity." *Scandinavian Journal of Management* 26, no. 4, pp. 439–47.

Stahl, G.K, M.L Maznevski, A. Voigt, and K. Jonsen. 2010. "Unraveling the Effects of Cultural Diversity in Teams: A Meta-Analysis of Research on Multicultural Work Groups." *Journal of International Business Studies* 41, no. 4, pp. 690–709.

Steffey, R.W., and V.S. Anantatmula. 2011. "International Projects Proposal Analysis: Risk Assessment Using Radial Maps." *Project Management Journal* 42, no. 3, pp. 62–74.

Sundstrom, E. 1999. "The Challenges of Supporting Work Team Effectiveness." In *Supporting Work Team Effectiveness,* 3–23. San Fransisco: Jossey-Bass.

Tajfel, H. 2010. *Social Identity and Intergroup Relations.* Cambridge: Cambridge University Press.

Thamhain, H.J. 2004. "Team Leadership Effectiveness in Technology-Based Project Environments." *Project Management Journal* 35, no. 4, pp. 35–46.

Theodore, G. 1971. "Taking the Sting out of Project Reassignment." *Management Review* 60, no. 1, pp. 54–57.

Thomas, M., P.H. Jacques, J.R. Adams, and J. Kihneman-Wooten. 2008. "Developing an Effective Project: Planning and Team Building Combined." *Project Management Journal* 39, no. 4, pp. 105–13.

Thomas, J., and T. Mengel. 2008. "Preparing Project Managers to Deal with Complexity—Advanced Project Management Education." *International Journal of Project Management* 26, no. 3, pp. 304–15.

Thompson, L. 2014. Making the Team: A Guide for Managers. 5th ed. NJ: Pearson.

Towers Watson. 2014. *2013–14 Communication and Change ROI Study Report.* New York: Towers Watson. www.towerswatson.com/en-US/Services/our-solutions/communication-and-change-management

Townsend, A.M., S.M. DeMarie, and A.R. Hendrickson. 1998. "Virtual Teams: Technology and the Workplace of the Future." *Academy of Management Executive* 12, no. 3, pp. 17–29.

Trevino, S., and V. Anantatmula. 2008. "Capitalizing from the Past Projects—The Value of Lessons Learned." In *Project Management Institute Research Conference.*

Trompenaars, A., and C. Hampden-Turner. 1998. *Riding the Waves of Culture: Understanding Diversity in Global Business.* New York: McGraw-Hill.

Tuckman, B. 1965. "Developmental Sequence in Small Groups." *Psychological Bulletin* 63, no. 6, pp. 384–99.

Turiera, T., and S. Cros. 2013. *Co Business: 50 Examples of Business Collaboration.* Barcelona, Spain: Infonomia.

Turner, R., and R. Muller. 2005. "The Project Manager's Role as a Success Factor on Projects: A Literature Review." *Project Management Journal* 36, no. 2, pp. 49–61.

Turner, R. 2006. "Matching the Project Manager's Leadership Style with the Project Type." *Lecture, PMI Research Conference*, Montreal, July 16.

Van den Bossche, P., W.H. Gijselaers, M. Segers, and P.A. Kirschner. 2006. "Social and Cognitive Factors Driving Teamwork in Collaborative Learning Environments: Team Learning Beliefs and Behaviors." *Small Group Research* 37, pp. 490–521.

Verma, V.K. 1995. *The Human Aspects of Project Management.* Upper Darby, PA: Project Management Institute.

Verma, V.K. 1996. *Human Resource Skills for the Project Manager.* Newtown Square, PA: Project Management Institute.

Villax, C., and V. Anantatmula. 2010. "Understanding and Managing Conflict in a Project Environment." *Lecture, PMI Education and Research Conference*, Washington, DC, July 12.

Wenger, E., and W. Snyder. 2000. "Communities of Practice: The Organizational Frontier." *Harvard Business Review* 78, no. 1, pp. 139–46.

West, M.A. 2004. *Effective Teamwork Practical Lessons from Organizational Research.* 2nd ed. Leicester: BPS Blackwell.

Whetten, D.A., and K.S. Cameron. 2007. *Developing Management Skills.* 6th ed. Upper Saddle River, NJ: Pearson/Prentice Hall.

Whetten, D.A., and K.S. Cameron. 2011. *Developing Management Skills.* 8th ed. Upper Saddle River, NJ: Prentice Hall.

WHO. 2009. Human Factors in Patient Safety Review of Topics and Tools: Report for Methods and Measures Working. *WHO Report.*

Wildman, J.L., and R. Griffith. 2015. *Leading Global Teams*. New York: Springer.

Wildman, J.L., A.L. Thayer, M.A. Rosen, E. Salas, J.E. Mathieu, and S.R. Rayne. 2012. "Task Types and Team-Level Attributes: Synthesis of Team Classification Literature." *Human Resource Development Review* 11, no. 1, pp. 97–129.

Yazici, H.J. 2009. "The Role of Project Management Maturity and Organizational Culture in Perceived Performance." *Project Management Journal* 40, no. 3, pp. 14–33.

Index

OTHER TITLES IN OUR PORTFOLIO AND PROJECT MANAGEMENT COLLECTION

Timothy Kloppenborg, Editor

- *Strategic Leadership of Portfolio and Project Management* by Timothy J. Kloppenborg and Laurence J. Laning
- *The Power of Design-Build: A Guide to Effective Design-Build Project Delivery Using the SAFEDB-Methodology* by Sherif Hashem
- *Information Systems Project Management* by David Olson
- *Leveraging Business Analysis for Project Success* by Vicki James
- *Project Portfolio Management: A Model for Improved Decision Making* by Clive N. Enoch
- *Project Management Essentials* by Kathryn Wells and Timothy J. Kloppenborg
- *The Agile Edge: Managing Projects Effectively Using Agile Scrum* by Brian Vanderjack

Announcing the Business Expert Press Digital Library

Concise e-books business students need for classroom and research

This book can also be purchased in an e-book collection by your library as

- a one-time purchase,
- that is owned forever,
- allows for simultaneous readers,
- has no restrictions on printing, and
- can be downloaded as PDFs from within the library community.

Our digital library collections are a great solution to beat the rising cost of textbooks. E-books can be loaded into their course management systems or onto students' e-book readers.
The **Business Expert Press** digital libraries are very affordable, with no obligation to buy in future years. For more information, please visit **www.businessexpertpress.com/librarians**. To set up a trial in the United States, please email **sales@businessexpertpress.com**.

CPSIA information can be obtained
at www.ICGtesting.com
Printed in the USA
FFOW02n1759210916
27735FF